D0936103

RETREATING FROM THE COLD WAR

Retreating from the Cold War

Germany, Russia and the Withdrawal of the Western Group of Forces

David Cox

Adjunct Professor of Political Science and International Affairs
The George Washington University

NEW YORK UNIVERSITY PRESS
Washington Square, New York

First published in the U.S.A. in 1996 by
NEW YORK UNIVERSITY PRESS
Washington Square
New York, N.Y. 10003

Library of Congress Cataloging-in-Publication Data
Cox, David, 1956–
Retreating from the cold war : Germany, Russia, and the withdrawal
of the Western Group of Forces / David Cox.
p.   cm.
Includes bibliographical references and index.
ISBN 0–8147–1528–1
1. Soviet Union—Military relations—Germany.   2. Germany-
-Military relations—Soviet Union.   3. Soviet Union.   Raboche
-Krest'ianskaia Krasnaia Armiia. Western Group of Forces.
4. Soviet Union—History—1985–1991.   5. Germany-
-History—1945–1990   I. Title.
DK68.7.G3C69   1996
327.47043'09'048—dc20   95–39395
                                                           CIP

Printed in Great Britain

For Carol

Contents

List of Maps and Tables

Maps

Table

Author's Note

This book is about the withdrawal of the former Soviet troops from what was East Germany. In a much larger sense, it is also about the end of the Cold War, as well as of the Soviet Union. All of these events were ultimately the result of Mikhail Gorbachev's reforms of Soviet society. They were not, however, entirely the intended consequences of his reforms.

Appropriately enough, the book did not turn out as originally intended either. What started out as separate analyses of different aspects of the withdrawal quickly became much more of a chronological narrative. While this may seem to make it more of a history and less political science, I hope it gives the book greater coherence and readability.

Hadia Samaha carried out a large part of the research for this book, while the Department of Political Science at The George Washington University provided financial support for the research assistance. Wendy Kolker proofread the manuscript and provided useful comments. I would also like to thank everyone at Macmillan and the New York University Press who helped in the production of this book.

The Russian language material was transliterated according to the system used by *The Current Digest of the Post-Soviet Press*. For simplicity's sake, all diacritical marks, whether in German, Russian or any of the other East European languages, were omitted.

DAVID COX

List of Abbreviations

CDU	*Christlich-Demokratische Union* (Christian Democratic Union)
CEMA	Council for Economic Mutual Assistance
CFE	Conventional Forces in Europe
CGF	Central Group of Forces
CIS	Commonwealth of Independent States
CPSU	Communist Party of the Soviet Union
CSCE	Conference on Security and Cooperation in Europe
FDP	*Freie Demokratische Partei* (Free Democratic Party)
FRG	Federal Republic of Germany
GDR	German Democratic Republic
GLCM	Ground Launched Cruise Missile
GSFG	Group of Soviet Forces in Germany
HSWP	Hungarian Socialist Workers' Party
INF	Intermediate-range Nuclear Forces
IRBM	Intermediate Range Ballistic Missile
KGB	*Komitet Gosudarstvennoi Bezopasnosti* (Committee for State Security)
MfS	*Ministerium für Staatssicherheit* (Ministry for State Security)
MPLA	*Movement Popular de Libertacão de Angola* (Popular Movement for the Liberation of Angola)
NATO	North Atlantic Treaty Organization
NGF	Northern Group of Forces
NVA	*Nationale Volksarmee* (National People's Army)
OMG	Operational Maneuver Group
PDPA	People's Democratic Party of Afghanistan
SDI	Strategic Defense Initiative
SED	*Sozialistische Einheitspartei Deutschlands* (Socialist Unity Party of Germany)
SGF	Southern Group of Forces
SMAG	Soviet Military Administration in Germany
SPD	*Sozialdemokratische Partei Deutschlands* (Social Democratic Party of Germany)
TVD	*Teatr Voyennikh Deystvy* (theater of military operations)

UN	United Nations
USSR	Union of Soviet Socialist Republics
WGF	Western Group of Forces
WTO	Warsaw Treaty Organization

1 The Politics of Decline

. . .a little patch of ground/That hath in it no profit but the name
  — William Shakespeare, *Hamlet*, Act IV, scene iv

The Soviet withdrawal from Germany was one of the most dramatic peacetime withdrawals in history. It was logistically on the same scale as the American deployment to Saudi Arabia during Operation Desert Shield. The withdrawal, as part of the general Soviet retreat from Eastern Europe, was largely the result of the USSR's inability to maintain its European military alliance, the Warsaw Treaty Organization (WTO). When Mikhail Gorbachev sought to increase the viability of the non-Soviet WTO states, he set into motion events that led to the Eastern European revolutions of 1989, which ended socialist rule in these countries.

By accepting pluralism and ruling out the use of force, Gorbachev undermined the socialist regimes in Eastern Europe and consequently Soviet hegemony over the region. Despite over forty years of socialist rule, both the regimes themselves and Soviet control ultimately rested on the presence or the threat of Soviet troops. The most important of these were the Soviet troops in East Germany, known as the Group of Soviet Forces in Germany, which was later redesignated as the Western Group of Forces (WGF). The WGF was the largest and most powerful of the Soviets' Groups of Forces in Eastern Europe[1] and, along with the East German army, represented the front-line units of the WTO.

The WGF also provided the last line of defense for socialist rule if the East German Communists were threatened with either foreign attack or internal opposition. In 1953, for example, the Soviet troops in East Germany had to be called in to suppress workers' riots in several cities.[2] Due to these offensive and defensive roles, the WGF was a focal point of the monumental changes that led to the end of the Cold War

1

and its withdrawal played a central role in German–Soviet foreign relations and continued to be a major issue between Germany and Russia until the final withdrawal on August 31, 1994.

In particular, the WGF played an important role in the 1989 East German revolution and subsequent reunification. Following Gorbachev's renunciation of the "Brezhnev Doctrine" of limited sovereignty for WTO states, the WGF did not intervene against the opposition forces during demonstrations against the socialist government of Erich Honecker. The Soviet troops even actively aided the East German opposition by advising their counterparts in the National People's Army not to intervene and even reportedly blocked East German troops inside their compounds.[3]

Following the installation of a reform government, which would lead to the beginnings of the reunification process, the status of the WGF quickly surfaced as a major issue in the discussions of the 2 + 4 Conference on German unification and bilateral West German–Soviet talks. As one of the concessions for Soviet acceptance of German unification and continued membership in the North Atlantic Treaty Organization (NATO), West Germany agreed to the continued deployment of the WGF on eastern German territory up to the end of 1994.[4] Further, the German government would pay for the maintenance costs of the WGF in eastern Germany, transportation costs to the Soviet border, and the construction of housing for the troops and their dependents in the USSR.

The withdrawal, as well as the Soviet withdrawals from Czechoslovakia, Hungary, and Poland, was also a major source of debate within the USSR. Hard-line communists and nationalists felt that Gorbachev and Eduard Shevardnadze, the Soviet foreign minister, were giving up the gains of World War II.[5] The withdrawals and the arms control agreements provided ammunition for the hard-liners, who criticized Gorbachev's policies, and whose attacks would later cause Shevardnadze to resign.

The WGF continues to play a major role in post-Soviet defense policy even after its dissolution. Like most of the rest of the Soviet Army, the WGF became part of the Joint Armed

Forces of the new Commonwealth of Independent States, but the command was quickly transferred to the Russian Army when it was re-established in May 1992. The WGF was considered to be "the most powerful and battleworthy grouping" of the Russian Army and its units would form the nucleus of the conventional forces following the completion of the withdrawal from Germany.[6]

This book, then, examines the politics surrounding the withdrawal of the WGF and its relation to the ending of the Cold War and the beginnings of the post-Cold War period. It looks at how the prior disengagement and the withdrawal itself relates to several different issues; including the 1989 East German revolution, German reunification, German–Soviet and German–Russian relations, and Russian domestic politics, including defense policy.

It will be argued that the withdrawal of the WGF was the result of the convergence of several factors which generally related to Gorbachev's reforms. The redefinition of Soviet security, changing economic and political relations in the USSR, the introduction of non-ideological concerns into Soviet foreign policy, and Soviet pressures on Eastern Europe to reform, all aided in the general dissolution of Soviet hegemony in Eastern Europe and, specifically, the collapse of socialism in East Germany.

The Soviet loss of hegemony in Eastern Europe was not, as has been argued, due to Western policies, but rather these internal changes in Soviet society. Moreover, the collapse of the Soviet "empire" in Europe was not entirely an unique historical occurrence. There have been numerous examples of states retreating from a region or regions, from the fall of the Roman Empire to the British pulling back from east of Aden. The collapse of the WTO is ultimately one case of this general pattern of the loss of hegemony.

THE COSTS OF HEGENOMY

Dominance of a system, whether political, economic, or social, obviously has its advantages. In addition to more immediate material gains, a dominant power, frequently referred to as a hegemon, typically reserves the right to determine what the rules of the system are. Consequently, it can structure those rules for its benefit, theoretically ensuring a positive benefits-to-costs ratio for maintaining the system. Having such a return is the underlying rationale for establishing the system in the first place.

Such concepts also apply to the international political system, which is most easily thought of as consisting "of a structure and of interacting units."[7] That is, a system is more than just the sum of its parts. There is some over-arching organization that limits and shapes the actions of the parts.[8] In the case of the international political system, this organization represents, at least in part, the rules of the system and much of international politics can be viewed as attempts to change some aspect of these rules.

Control over the international system has been considered as analogous to a domestic political system, although the international one is more anarchic. National authority, or sovereignty, relies on five, somewhat interrelated, components: a government, authority, property rights, law, and the domestic economy.[9] While less absolute, control over an international system rests on five corresponding mechanisms: dominance of the great powers, a hierarchy of prestige, division of territory, the rules of the systems, and the international economy.[10]

In general, there has been three types of control of the international system, all of which are based on how power is distributed within the system. The first is an unipolar system where one actor dominates the other actors in the system. An unipolar system can either be imperial, where one actor physically occupies the other actors, or hegemonic, which is where one actor dominates the system.[11] The second type is a bipolar structure, where there are two actors controlling their respective spheres of influence. The third means of control is a multipolar system, where a number of actors balance each other off.[12]

In all three cases, the most powerful actors determine the basic outlines of the system, including the nature of the actors, the governance of the system, and the types of interactions.[13]

None of these factors are static, however, and changes in the relative capabilities of the actors can bring pressures for changing the system. If a secondary actor gains power relative to the dominant actor, it may want to change some part of the system for its own benefit. If these changes relate to the processes within the system, it can be thought of as an interaction change. A change in the governing of the system is a systemic change, while a change in the nature of the actors would be a systems change.[14]

There is, then, quite a lot to be gained from controlling a system. In the case of international politics, one could literally rule the world. There are, however, numerous costs associated with the benefits of hegemony. In the first place, one must achieve this dominance. Since this view of the international political system is based on power, an actor must have sufficient resources, organization, and will to achieve the necessary measure of control. An attempt to achieve dominance or pre-eminence also means that the actor is not employing these attributes in some other fashion, which represents an opportunity cost to the actor.[15]

A successful attempt would generally imply that the dominant power had some sort of superiority over the other units. Many of the initial expansions of international actors, whether a city-state, an empire, or a nation-state, have historically taken place because of such a superiority.[16] The negative side of this superiority is that the dominant power has to maintain a level of superiority over other actors or risk challenges by them.[17] Once again, resources are directed towards control of the system, but now in a potentially unending process.

This interaction is part of the underlying logic of a international political process that has become known as "long cycles." Long cycles are based on recurrent patterns of rise and decline by major powers, or power transitions, within the international system. The dominant power, for numerous possible reasons, slowly loses its ability to keep the system together and, when faced with a challenger who is at least perceived to be stronger if not actually so, is forced into a major war over control of the system.[18]

These global wars represent fundamental shifts in the international system. The Thirty Years' War (1618–48), for example, traditionally marks the beginnings of the modern nation-state system. Their cyclical nature, however, means that a new dominant power is faced with the same sort of pattern as the power they replaced. This pattern consists of four distinct phases: global war, world power, delegitimation and deconcentration.[19] After a global war, the winning power can structure the international order, becoming the dominant world power. Delegitimation, brought on by the relative decline of the world power, is the beginning of the breakdown of this order, while the final stage, deconcentration, is marked by a challenge to the hegemon.[20]

While there are more deterministic schools of thought on the process of systems change, such as Kondratrieff waves, which focuses on long-term changes in the international economy, ultimately, some decision maker has to make an analysis that it is their interest to change the system. Unless the leaders of a state (or empire or city-state) believe that the expected benefits of changing the international system outweigh the potential costs of doing so, the system will remain relatively stable.[21] A stable system is not without its own costs, however, as the powers which have the most interest in the continuance of that system have to be willing to pay a disproportionate share of the costs of that system.[22]

If an actor does believe that the benefits will outweigh the costs, then it will attempt such a change. It will attempt to expand territorial, politically or economically until it reaches an equilibrium between costs and benefits.[23] Once it has reached this point of equilibrium, however, the law of diminishing returns takes over and the costs of maintaining the new status quo rise faster than the benefits, which can create a new disequilibrium and a new challenger may set out to redress the balance.[24]

A challenger for the control of the system also incurs costs. Since it is taking on the pre-eminent power, it will most likely seek like-minded allies to aid it in the conflict. The challenger is then not only in the position of confronting the dominant power but also being the leader of the opposition coalition.

This was the position the USSR found itself in during the post-World War II ideological struggle known as the Cold War. As the challenger to the dominant power, the United States, the USSR sought, at least ultimately, to reshape the international system through the final victory of socialism over capitalism. This transition would also lead to the end of nation-states as the principal international actors.

In addition, the USSR was also the "leading socialist state," since it was the first such state, and positioned itself as the head of what used to be called the socialist community. From the Soviets' point of view, the second most important part of these socialist forces were the countries of Eastern Europe. The Red Army's liberation of the region during the final stages of World War II provided Joseph Stalin with the opportunity to install friendly regimes in these states, thereby breaking the USSR's international isolation.

It also made the USSR the hegemonic power in the region as the Soviets dominated the domestic and foreign politics of the non-Soviet WTO countries. The Eastern European states adopted the Soviet system of state socialism and were ruled by leaders who were loyal to Stalin. They joined the WTO, while their militaries were closely integrated with the Soviet Army. In effect, the WTO states amounted to a subsystem of the international system, one that the Soviets were willing to pay for to maintain their hegemony.

OVEREXTENSION AND DECLINE

As noted above, a state that believes it is in its interest to organize the international system is therefore willing to pay the costs of that system. As long as no other state is willing to challenge that system, then the international system is in a state of equilibrium.[25] This does not mean that a state of dominance, hegemony, or pre-eminence is static, however. Numerous factors can change the relations between the members of the systems, leading a rising, and dissatisfied, power to attempt to change the system.

These factors, which range from economic, political, societal, strategic to technological, all relate to a potential decline in the power of the dominant state. Such a decline is not necessarily an absolute decline, since a state can continue to expand, but rather it has to be a relative decline in comparison to the rising power.[26] In other words, both powers could be expanding, but the challenger would be doing so at a faster rate, giving the impression of a decline in the power of the hegemon. Relative decline is not necessarily a problem unless the rising state is also dissatisfied with the established system and wishes to revise it somehow.

It is possible for a pre-eminent power to lose its standing within the system without showing any internal sign of decline. The Chinese Qing Dynasty of the eighteenth century, for example, simply fell behind the technology being developed in Western Europe, despite having a much larger and growing economy than the United Kingdom, which was expanding its empire into Asia.[27] It this case, it was a relative qualitative change that led to the downfall of the Chinese hegemony in East Asia.

In the case of the Qing Empire, it was an extraneous factor that led to its decline. The Industrial Revolution was not something they could have necessarily foreseen and consequently made different policy choices. Other dominant powers have lost their position due to domestic choices that, in the long run, diminished their capabilities to led. The imperial bureaucracy and the large standing armies of the Roman Empire in the West ultimately became too costly in comparison to its ability to raise revenue, which led to its increasing inability to defend itself from numerous border tribes.[28]

The nature of a society can influence national power. A status quo-oriented political system can hinder new solutions to problems. If, for example, special or vested interests dominate the domestic political agenda with the intent of safeguarding their budgetary position, then a country's economic well-being could be negatively affected. Such "distributional coalitions" can also block initiative and prevent new technologies from being introduced.[29]

In other cases, domestic policies are affected by the international situation. A country can choose to deal with foreign commitments at the expense of domestic problems. The principal, and highly debated, example cited is the present-day United States. The American economy has been seen by some analysts as losing its international competitiveness, largely due to its military expenditures and large public debt.[30] A declining economy can also be compounded by societal factors, such as the decline in American education or excessive domestic consumption.[31]

The case of the American hegemony is closely related to, and is largely a special case of, the principal cause of decline, which is an international overcommitment of resources. This overextension is known as "imperial" or "strategic overstretch."[32] Overstretch can occur through establishing a large empire, whether formal or informal, or fighting a series of costly wars, or some combination of both. An overreaching power ultimately reaches a point where it simply can no longer afford its hegemony due to economic or strategic factors.

Because economic wealth and military power are closely interrelated, strategic overstretch is closely tied to the state of a country's economic base. Extensive foreign commitments, however, can take up too much of a percentage of the national income, especially governmental revenues. The "burden of empire," or the costs of maintaining an international system or subsystem, typically become too expensive when it reaches 10 percent or more of a country's gross national product.[33] Overextension also negatively affects the economy as resources are diverted from research and development, thereby exacerbating the decline.

There have been several historical examples of strategic overstretch. The first modern attempt at achieving hegemony over Europe was the efforts of the Austrian and Spanish Hapsburgs in the seventeenth century, which culminated in the Thirty Years' War. The Hapsburg Empire simply had too many enemies to overcome, however, and was ultimately forced to accept religious diversity and political decentralization on the continent. The French, who initially gained the most from the defeat of the Hapsburgs, would later overextend themselves as well in a series of wars, the last one being the Napoleonic Wars. Like the Hapsburgs, the French were defeated by a coalition opposed to the establishment of hegemony in Europe.

Both the Netherlands and Sweden also gained from the Spanish defeat. The newly-independent Netherlands would establish a far-flung trading empire, which briefly made it the major economic power in Europe. The Swedish dominated the Baltic Sea region, creating their own empire in northern Europe. Probably the most famous example of imperial overstretch, however, was the British Empire. Despite their relatively small population and national economy, the British physically conquered much of the world and dominated the international system, ensuring open access to foreign markets. It was eventually overtaken by both Germany and the United States, which were newer, more dynamic industrial powers. In all these cases, global or major wars led not only to an end to hegemony but also to a loss of colonial territory by the former major power.

In retrospect, it seems almost too obvious that the USSR had strategically overextended itself.[34] The costs of confronting the United States around the world, maintaining a military alliance in Europe, matching American defense spending with an economic base less than half the size, and supporting socialist-leaning Third World states, all took their toll on Soviet resources. Later estimates of Soviet defense spending ranged from seventeen or eighteen percent to twenty-five percent of the Soviet national product.[35]

To compound the costs of the military competition, the Soviet economy had been experiencing a declining growth rate since the 1960s, when it had reached the limits of extensive growth. The centralized command economy never adapted to the needs of intensive growth, while the co-optation policies of Leonid Brezhnev ensured high budgetary priorities for defense and heavy industry at the expense of investment and especially non-defense related research and development. Brezhnev also tended to put off difficult decisions that might have jeopardized his rule. The resulting "stagnation" led to an economic state of "pre-crisis" in the USSR.[36]

The combination of military commitments and economic problems meant that by the mid-1980s the USSR had seriously overextended itself. By taking on the United States, with its larger economy and richer allies, the Soviets had misjudged what they referred to as the "correlation of forces," which had appeared to be in socialism's favor following the establishment of communist regimes in Eastern Europe and Asia after World War II. They had, as one observer noted, "begun to swallow the world . . . and then realized just how big the world is."[37]

ADAPTION STRATEGIES

While no state can hope to achieve permanent hegemony, the process of decline does not necessarily appear to be irreversible or inevitable, at least in the short run. Several states or empires have managed to maintain their position as the dominant power for extended periods of time through changes in policy or reforms. Other states have adapted to the change in international power and accepted, either quietly or not so quietly, second-rank status. In the first case, the dominant power affected a renewal of its international position, while the second case represents a definite decline.

Many formerly dominant states and challengers accepted their loss in status. Sweden, the main supporter of the Protestant cause in the Thirty Years' War and the main power in the Baltic after the war, never sought to regain its holdings in the region following its defeat in the Great Northern War. The Netherlands relatively peacefully accepted Britain's rise to power. Both the Japanese and the West Germans largely turned to business after their defeats in World War II.

The British also had to adjust to their loss of status. While some have never completely accepted the loss of the empire, Britain allowed many of its former colonies to become independent in the years after World War II. The British also moved from relying on military or diplomatic means to influence its former colonies to economics.[38] Other states have attempted to maintain their international position, despite the rise of a new dominant power or challenger, through increased cooperation with potential rivals, a practice referred to as hegemonic stability.[39]

Alternately, a state can seek to pre-empt its decline through the military defeat of its challenger. A preventive war strategy is, of course, very risky. In the Thirty Years' War, for example, the Spanish launched an invasion of France, Spain's principal rival in the conflict, as a means of resolving the deadlocked war. The Spanish first minister, Olivares, stated that "either all is lost, or else Castile will be head of the world."[40] The Spanish decision to come to the aid the Austrian Hapsburgs was based in part on the tactical superiority of the Spanish infantry, which was the considered to be the best in the Europe.[41]

While the Spanish did achieve several notable military victories, the most famous being the battle of Nordlingen, ultimately they were worn down by fighting on numerous fronts. Even though they even managed to keep fighting the French for several years after the end of the Thirty Years' War in 1648, the cost of the conflicts drained the Spanish treasury.[42] Spain would never recover its previous status after the defeat. A preemptive strategy has also been cited as one of the causes of World War I. The Germans, concerned about fighting a two-front war, in effect decided to go to war while their technical superiority was still intact.[43]

At best, a preemptive strategy would only be a short-term solution. To prevent further decline, a state would have to address the fundamental causes of that decline. The principal means of doing so is through reform. Both the Roman and Chinese empires, for example, managed to introduce innovations that continued their superiority over their respective rivals. At a point in time when the Roman Empire might have begun to collapse, Augustus Caesar reformed the imperial bureaucracy, which allowed for the further expansion of the empire.[44] Various Chinese dynasties successfully modernized the economy and technology before ultimately falling behind the European states.[45]

Nation-states can similarly change policies that are contributing to their decline. In a very broad sense, state leaders are faced with a choice of providing security or welfare for the country.[46] This choice is not necessarily an either/or proposition as states actually seek a combination of the two, one that maximizes both.[47] A state which has overextended itself could decrease its military burden, through either a reduction of foreign commitments, cutting the military budget, or seeking allies to share the defense burden.

Alternately, a state could introduce policies which attempt to redress the decline, without giving up hegemony. A more draconian strategy would entail a decrease in public welfare expenditures to finance the military, leading to a highly militarized state. Alternately, a state can adopt policies that would add to its resources, such as liberal immigration, free trade, or measures to ensure continued competitiveness.[48]

In this light, Gorbachev's reforms of *glasnost* (openness), *demokratizatsiya* (democratization), and *perestroika* (restructuring) could be viewed as a means of Soviet renewal. He actually even referred to his reforms as a socialist renewal. Gorbachev wanted to increase Soviet productivity, especially the introduction of new technology, and to increase popular participation in politics to overcome the stagnation of the later Brezhnev years. At a minimum, he seems to have wanted to provide the USSR with *peredyshka* (breathing space) to allow it to catch up with the West, if not to fundamentally transform Soviet society.

The reduction of the Soviets' relative military burden was an integral part of his reforms. Gorbachev sought to limit military spending in relation to the amounts the Soviets spent on consumption and investment.[49] In effect, Gorbachev attempt to shift the balance between security and welfare in the USSR as a means to prevent a further erosion in Soviet power. At the same time, he also wanted to reduce the possible threats to the USSR, and hence the need to counter those threats, through diplomacy. The foreign policy aspects of his reforms would become known as new political thinking.

Gorbachev's reforms also affected Eastern Europe. They were expected to participate in the economic restructuring of the Soviet economy, but, at the same time, Gorbachev wanted to decrease Soviet expenses for the region. He was willing to reduce the Soviet military presence in Europe and wanted the Soviet allies to be more self-sufficient by introducing Eastern European versions of *perestroika*. Gorbachev's reform efforts took on a life of their own, however, and ultimately led to the establishment of independent governments and the Soviet military disengagement from the region.

OVERVIEW

The collapse of the Eastern European socialist regimes marked the end of the Cold War.[50] Consequently, the circumstances surrounding the withdrawal of the WGF represent a microcosm of the end of the Cold War. While the case of the WGF is somewhat unique, since East Germany would later unify with a NATO member-state, it reflects the general pattern of the withdrawals from what was known as the Soviets' "Outer Empire."[51] As would follow then, the work is a case study of the withdrawal of the WGF. Generally, it deals with both Soviet and Russian domestic debates and relations between Moscow and the various Germanies over the WGF. Specifically, it looks at the changing force posture and structure of the WGF and how they were affected by domestic and foreign policies.

The study consists of seven chapters which generally relate to the major issues. Chapter 1 deals with the more theoretical concerns of hegemony and strategic overstretch and how these concepts applied to the Soviets. Chapter 2 looks at the role of East Germany and the WGF within the Soviet alliance system until the beginnings of Gorbachev's reforms. Chapter 3 examines Gorbachev's new political thinking in foreign affairs and how it related to the WTO in general and the WGF specifically.

Chapter 4 covers the events of 1989 in East Germany and the role of the WGF in the revolution. Chapter 5 looks at German–Soviet relations over the WGF and unification and withdrawal, as well as German–Russian relations over the continuing withdrawal. Chapter 6 deals with Soviet and

Russian domestic politics concerning the withdrawal and Chapter 7 will provide conclusions about the entire process.

The primary sources for this work were the Soviet, and later Russian press reports, as well as German accounts. Given the extensive coverage of these events, there were also numerous Western scholarly analyses and more popular accounts that provided background information and insights.

2 The GDR, GSFG and WTO

Armed at point exactly, cap-à-pé
— William Shakespeare, *Hamlet*, Act I, scene ii

The concept of strategic overstretch somewhat obviously implies that a state has made too many international commitments in relation to its resources. The fundamental choice for an overextended power then is what interests are central and hence to be held onto and which can be abandoned because they are not worth the costs. For the Soviets, there was simply no question that Eastern Europe was paramount to their conception of national security. Of these countries, the German Democratic Republic (GDR) was probably their most important ally in the Cold War. The GDR was, with some notable exceptions, one of the strongest supporters of Soviet foreign policy, had one of the most modern armies among the non-Soviet WTO states, and most importantly, provided the USSR with a forward base for the Soviet Army. At the same time, the costs of maintaining the socialist regimes in Eastern Europe were very high.

This chapter will examine the interrelations between the GDR, the USSR, and the WTO up until the beginnings of Gorbachev's reforms. It will look at the history of Soviet involvement in Eastern Europe, the establishment of the GDR and WTO, the force posture and structure of the Soviet and East German militaries, and the changes in Soviet policies in the 1970s and early 1980s. One of the focal points of this involvement was the WGF.

WORLD WAR II ANTECEDENTS

Appropriately enough, the story of what would eventually become the WGF began in World War II, or, as the Soviets called it, the Great Patriotic War. Following the 1941 German *blitzkrieg*, which overran the Baltic republics, Byelorussia, and the Ukraine and reached the city limits of both Leningrad and Moscow, the Soviets eventually regrouped and launched a limited counterattack against the German Army Group Center in December, which ended the immediate threat to the Soviet capital.

By 1942, the Germans simply did not have the resources to attack along the entire Eastern front. Consequently, Adolf Hitler, the German leader, decided to seize the southern industrial area of Donets and the oil fields at Baku in the Caucasus.[1] In addition to decreasing the Soviet war-making potential, such a move would also supply Germany with much-needed oil. Army Group South was reorganized into two commands, Army Group A, which was to head for the Caucasus, and Army Group B, which was to provide flank cover for Group A.[2] The Germans overcame the Soviet defenses near the city of Voronezh in June 1942 and, in a near replay of the previous summer, raced towards their objectives.

Unlike in 1941, however, the Germans were not capturing large numbers of Red Army prisoners. This time, the Soviets were pulling back in a relatively orderly manner. The retreat reached a natural barrier at Stalingrad, however, since the Volga river was a major transportation line when it was ice-free. In addition, there were also psychological motivations to hold the city named after the Soviet leader. Stalin issued an order to General Vassily Chuykov, the commander of the 62d Army, that the city was to be held at all costs.[3]

It was at the battle for Stalingrad that the Soviet forces would begin their long road to Germany. Chuykov's army managed to hold on to a bridgehead in the city, while a Soviet counteroffensive, *Operatsiya Uran* (Operation Uranus), was prepared. On November 19, 1942, the Red Army attacked the German allied forces, which included Hungarian, Italian, and Romanian troops, on the flanks of Army Group B. The Soviet troops quickly overran these largely inferior units and surrounded the German 6th Army in Stalingrad. Despite a German relief effort, Field Marshal von Paulus, the commander of the 6th Army, surrendered in February 1943.

The Soviet victory at Stalingrad was a major defeat for the Germans. They lost much of their armored strength on the Eastern front and suffered over 300,000 casualties in the battle. Some of the German prisoners would become Marxists during their captivity and would later form the nucleus of the East German army.[4] For the Soviets, Stalingrad represented a psychological turning point. From now on, they would largely be heading west instead of retreating east.[5]

The Germans would launch one more major summer offensive against the Soviet positions around the city of Kursk. In bitter positional fighting more reminiscent of World War I, which featured the largest tank battle of the war, the Soviets held their ground and then launched a counter-offensive which cleared the eastern Ukraine. After Kursk, the war in the east largely settled into a series of Soviet advances, which consisted of a general pattern of river-to-river operations.[6]

As for what would become the WGF, Chuykov was promoted after Stalingrad and given the command of the 8th Guards Army. It was involved in the Kursk battle and the subsequent westward advances, including Operation Bagration, named after one of the heroes of the 1812 war against Napoleon, in 1944, which resulted in the near-destruction of the German Army Group Center. In the subsequent Soviet advance, Chuykov's army would liberate the Polish city of Lublin, which provided Stalin with the opportunity to establish a communist-led Polish government.[7]

The 8th Guards Army would also play a central role in the final operations against the Germans. Chuykov's force was part of Marshal Georgy Zhukov's 1st Belorussian Front, which was positioned to capture the German capital of Berlin. In January 1945, the Soviets launched an offensive from their Vistula river beachheads and raced across Poland. Chuykov's forces reached the banks of the Oder river near Berlin in February, but Zhukov had outrun his flank support. Rather than marching on the German capital as Chuykov wanted,[8] the 1st Belorussian cleared out German units in the Baltic region of Pomerania, while Marshal Ivan Konyev's 1st Ukrainian Front advanced into Silesia.

The Soviets then turned to Berlin itself. Zhukov's and Konyev's forces surrounded and then fought their way into the city. Zhukov accepted the formal German surrender or May 9, 1945. After the war, he became the high commissioner of Soviet-occupied Germany, chief of the Soviet Military Administration in Germany (SMAG), and a member of the Allied Control Commission for occupied Berlin. He was also named the commander-in-chief of the Soviet troops in Germany.[9] This command, which largely consisted of Zhukov's 1st Belorussian Front, marked the beginning of the WGF.

AN UNUSUAL EMPIRE

The Soviet victory over Nazi Germany also meant that the USSR physically occupied most of the states of Eastern Europe. Stalin, however, viewed World War II as different from other wars in that "whoever occupies a territory also imposes on it his own social system. Everyone imposes his own social system as far as his army can reach."[10] With Red Army troops either present or nearby, pro-Soviet communists set about gaining political power and adopting Soviet policies throughout Eastern Europe.

The Soviets relied on several control mechanisms for the newly-founded "People's Democracies" of Eastern Europe. Soviet ambassadors to these countries frequently acted more as imperial viceroys than diplomats. Their armies were reformed along Soviet lines, complete with political officers and Soviet advisers,[11] while the USSR signed bilateral defense treaties with the countries. Soviet personnel would also oversee the activities of other governmental bodies, including the security services. In addition, Stalin placed communist party members who had spent the war years in Moscow as the heads of the east European parties over local, potentially more nationalist, party leaders.

The Soviets seized East European assets as war reparations from several of the countries, with most of these reparations coming from the Soviet occupation zone in Germany. The Soviets also established what were called joint stock companies in many of the new socialist states. These companies were Soviet-controlled and represented a more indirect means of aiding the Soviet post-war recovery. They were so blatantly exploitative that Stalin dissolved them in the late 1940s.

The various Soviet actions in Eastern Europe were one of the major causes of the Cold War. From Stalin's point of view, however, the establishment of Soviet hegemony in Eastern Europe was worth the confrontation with the United States. Ideologically, the near-isolation of the USSR was finally broken, thereby making good on Stalin's promise that his autarkic policy of "Socialism in One Country" was merely temporary. The addition of these new allies also constituted a significant gain in the correlation of forces for socialism.

The geopolitical gains were just as important, if not more so. Stalin now controlled the heart of Europe, which would become a buffer zone to prevent another Western invasion of the USSR. It also provided the Soviets a means to threaten American interests in Western Europe if the United States decided to use its nuclear monopoly against the USSR. The Soviet troops in Eastern Europe, and particularly the troops in Germany, were in effect the first, and very rudimentary, Soviet strategic deterrent force.[12]

The Soviet position in Eastern Europe also effectively divided the continent in two. The infamous "Iron Curtain" was established to keep the socialist side socialist. Given the Soviets' obsession with secrecy, Western access to the region was minimized. Consequently, the American offer of economic assistance through the Marshall Plan was turned down, even though Czechoslovakia and Poland had both expressed interest. As an alternative to the rejected American offer, Stalin created the Council for Economic Mutual Assistance (CEMA) in 1949 to coordinate economic activity within the Soviet sphere. CEMA, however, would remain largely a paper organization until after Stalin's death in 1953.[13]

Stalin was the linchpin of the Soviet system, both in the USSR and in Eastern Europe. Stalin clearly subordinated Eastern Europe to Soviet interests, preferring Stalinist governments over more viable, but potentially more independent, nationalists. When Stalin died on March 6, 1953, both the USSR and Eastern Europe had to deal with the ensuing succession crisis. Demonstrations broke out in Czechoslovakia and the GDR that summer. The Czechoslovak riots were put down by Czechoslovak police, but, as noted, the Soviet Army had to be called out to suppress the protests in East Germany.

Within the Communist Party of the Soviet Union (CPSU), Nikita Khrushchev eventually won out over his principal challenger, Georgy Malenkov. Khrushchev would later seek to distance himself from Stalin's policies and begin a de-Stalinization program in the USSR. Khrushchev's attacks on Stalin and Soviet acceptance of Yugoslavia's independent path to socialism, however, undermined the authority of the East European leaders, most of whom were still committed Stalinists.

The lack of legitimacy of the Eastern European parties would come to a head in October 1956. In Poland, Wladyslaw Gomulka, a nationalist party member, had succeeded in gaining the leadership of the Polish United Workers' Party, the communist-led front organization, and proceeded to introduce reforms, including freedom of religion. When Khrushchev threatened to intervene militarily, Gomulka countered with a threat to call out the Polish people.[14] Khrushchev backed down from intervening in exchange for Polish acceptance of Soviet foreign policy.

The Polish crisis was barely over before nationalists in Hungary succeeded in overthrowing Matyas Rakosi, the Stalinist leader of the Hungarian Communist Party. Unlike in Poland, however, the nationalists were not satisfied with the independence of the party and began to introduce Western-style political reforms and sought Hungary's withdrawal from the recently-established WTO. These reforms proved to be too much for the Soviets and they invaded in force. The Hungarian Revolution was violently put down and the renamed communist party, the Hungarian Socialist Workers' Party (HSWP), was returned to power.

Despite Khrushchev's willingness to use force to maintain socialist regimes in Eastern Europe, he realized that he needed more responsive means to keep Eastern Europe bound to the USSR. His solution was to use the multilateral organizations that had been established earlier. CEMA was resurrected and used to tie the economies of the region to the USSR's. Five-year plans were coordinated and, to a limited extent, integrated, although Khrushchev had to back down from his plans at greater integration.[15]

Khrushchev also wanted to bind the East European armies to the USSR. He signed Status of Forces treaties with the countries that had Soviet troops to legitimize their presence[16] and began to rely more on the Warsaw Pact as a means of defense and foreign policy integration. The WTO was established after West Germany's admittance to NATO in 1955 but initially it too was largely a paper organization, although it did provide justification for the presence of Soviet troops in Hungary after the Soviet withdrawal from Austria that same year.

The WTO was created by the Warsaw Treaty of 1955, which was signed by Albania, Bulgaria, Czechoslovakia, Hungary, Poland, Romania, and the USSR, while the GDR joined the pact the following year. The primary structures of the WTO consisted of a Political Consultative Committee, composed of the party leaders of the members, a Council of the Foreign Ministers, and a High Command of the Joint Armed Forces. The High Command was headquartered in Moscow and the commander-in-chief of the Joint Armed Forces was always a Soviet officer. All of the Soviet Groups of Forces in Eastern Europe were assigned to the Joint Armed Forces of the WTO.

Both CEMA and the WTO were largely Soviet-dominated and demonstrated the costs the Soviets were willing to pay to maintain both the other socialist regimes and their hegemony in the region. The Soviets, for example, paid approximately eighty percent of the costs associated with the WTO and provided sixty percent of the forces assigned to the pact. In comparison, the United States paid sixty percent of the costs of NATO and provided 42 percent of the troops.[17]

The Soviets, especially under Stalin, were willing to pay these costs for military reasons. Even as the Cold War grew in intensity, the Soviets proved willing to accept limited ideological reforms within the parties, but would not accept neutrality, as the events in Poland and Hungary in 1956 demonstrated.[18] Soviet military doctrine called for a coalition war to carry out a decisive offensive. The first requirement was Eastern European participation. The policy also all but necessitated a common border with NATO, which was one of the reasons why the GDR was so important to the USSR.

THE 16TH REPUBLIC

When the wartime allies agreed in 1944 to establish separate occupation zones in Germany and Berlin, they never intended for the division to permanent. The wartime cooperation, however, quickly turned into post-war suspicion and the country was effectively divided. In both eastern and western Germany, the victors sought to establish a new social system based on their respective ideologies. The Western allies relied on pro-Western German politicians in their occupation government, while the Soviets used German communists to assist the SMAG.

One of these communists was Walter Ulbricht, who spent the war in Moscow and followed the Red Army into Berlin. By 1950, he was named as general secretary of the *Sozialistische Einheitspartei Deutschlands* (SED), or the Socialist Unity Party of Germany, which had been created earlier through the merger of German communists and social democrats, along with some smaller, mostly leftist parties, in the Soviet zone.

As the Cold War heated up, the possibility of a reunited Germany became less and less likely. The Western allies allowed their zones to merge into the Federal Republic of Germany (FRG), or West Germany, in 1949. A federal parliamentary system was established by the *Grundgesetz* (Basic Law), which was, in theory, to serve as the FRG's temporary constitution. The Basic Law did not recognize the division of Germany and provided two measures for reunification: Article 23, which allowed for German territories as of 1937 to accede to the Basic Law; and Article 41, which called for the establishment of a new constitution representing the new constituent parts.

The Soviets responded to the establishment of the FRG by creating the GDR out of their zone, including their sector of Berlin, in October 1949. East Berlin was named the capital of the GDR. The SED was ensured of the leadership of the government by the 1949 East German constitution.[19] A Soviet-style party-state was set up, complete with East German versions of Soviet institutions, with the notable exception of an army. Instead, the Soviets established a frontier force, which was later reorganized as the *Kasernierte Volkspolizei* (People's Police in Barracks).[20]

When Stalin's last attempt at reuniting Germany failed, the Soviets turned their attentions to establishing the GDR as a sovereign state. The occupation status of the Soviet troops in Germany was abrogated by the USSR in 1954[21] and a treaty on the stationing of Soviet forces in the GDR was signed on March 12, 1957. This treaty gave the commander of the Soviet troops wide latitude to maintain the security of his troops.[22] The Soviets also allowed East Germany to establish its own army, the *Nationale Volksarmee* (NVA), or the National People's Army, in 1956.

The NVA was, aside from its uniforms, a virtual copy of the Soviet Army. It was organized along Soviet lines, with air defence forces, border guards, land forces, a navy, and other specialized units. It was equipped with Soviet arms and its table of ranks largely corresponded to Soviet grades.[23] East German soldiers received intensive political indoctrination, which was supervised by the East German Main Political Administration. The GDR also established a militia force, the *Kampfgruppen der Arbeiterklasse* (Combat Units of the Working Class) under the authority of the Ministry of the Interior.[24]

More importantly than the organizational resemblance, the NVA was, for all intents and purposes, an adjunct of the Soviet Army. Unlike the other WTO members, the entire NVA was assigned to the Joint Armed Forces of the pact. The East German air force, which was separate from the air defence forces, was under virtual Soviet control. Soviet

officials routinely supervised their GDR counterparts, but the
Soviet Army had a formal position, the deputy commander-
in-chief of the Joint Forces of the Warsaw Pact in the NVA,
within the East German military.[25]

The East German intelligence services also closely mirrored
their Soviet counterparts and were similarly under tight
control. The *Ministerium fur Staatssicherheit* (MfS), or the
Ministry for State Security, cooperated with the Soviet KGB,
which relied heavily on the MfS to infiltrate West Germany.
The MfS also monitored both East German citizens and the
NVA. The KGB kept a close watch on the GDR, however. It
operated almost openly on GDR territory, recruiting East
German citizens to work for them, and could issue orders to
both the MfS and the police. This high degree of penetration
led KGB officers to refer to the GDR as "the 16th Republic of
the USSR."[26]

COMRADESHIP-IN-ARMS

As noted, Stalin opted for a high level of cohesion among the
East European allies. Khrushchev, on the other hand, allowed
for some measure of viability for the WTO states after the
Hungarian Revolution. He even encouraged reforms within
the system that corresponded to his own efforts in the USSR.
On defense issues, however, the Soviets sought to bind the
East European armies as closely as possible to Soviet doctrine
and strategy.

To achieve this integration, the Soviets relied on a near-
monopoly on equipment and training for the rest of the WTO.
Aside from licensed production of Soviet weapons and some
independent production, most of the armaments in the
Warsaw Pact forces were Soviet-built. Soviet control over
weapons deliveries meant that they had significant influence
over the quality of an allied military. The NVA, for example,
was consistently upgraded in terms of the quality of weapons
it received and by the 1970s was among the first WTO armies
to get next-generation equipment from the USSR.[27]

Eastern European officers were trained in Soviet doctrine and military art and would then pass the Soviet methods on to their recruits. These officers were the key point of control for the Soviets over the WTO armies, since the recruits were simply expected to do what they were told. To make sure the officers would fight alongside the Soviets, East European officers were subject to the same sort of political controls that existed in the Soviet Army. They were, for example, generally expected to join the communist party and anyone who wished to advance in rank sought higher command training at the Voroshilov Academy in Moscow.

The Soviets also conducted frequent joint exercises with most of the rest of the WTO forces. In addition to the military training, these exercises were intended to promote comradeship for the "fraternal armies." These mechanisms effectively limited the options of the non-Soviet WTO armies. Their weapons were Soviet, their officers Soviet-trained, and their units configured to fight a Soviet-style war. WTO doctrine called for joint operations under an unified command, which in practice meant that non-Soviet units would have likely been "corseted" by Soviet units to prevent independent action. If a war broke out, they would have had little choice but to follow the Soviets into battle, which was largely the Soviets' intentions.[28]

The Romanians, however, began to distance themselves from WTO doctrine in the 1960s. They went outside the WTO for some of their military equipment, buying helicopters from France and, later, patrol boats from the Chinese. They also entered into an agreement with the Yugoslavs to co-produce a jet fighter, the *Orao* (Eagle). Most importantly, they reconfigured their units for a territorial defense and refused to allow either Soviet units or WTO troop exercises in Romania. In addition, they would also adopt a more independent foreign policy line, both within the WTO and in dealing with non-socialist countries.

The Soviets accepted this independence partly because Romania was capable of at least offering resistance to an intervention due to their adoption of a territorial defense strategy. But since Romania remained under strict communist party control, to the point that they even retained the Stalinist model, there was little reason for the Soviets to intervene. As it turned out, the first major crisis of the WTO was not Romania's growing independence or Albania's earlier defection, but the emergence of a reform movement in Czechoslovakia.

Czechoslovak Communist Party reformers forced out Antonin Novotny, the hard-line first secretary, and replaced him with the head of the Slovak Communist Party, Alexander Dubcek, in January 1968. Dubcek's new government wanted to adopt "socialism with a human face" as a means of gaining legitimacy. In the first months of 1968, the Czechoslovak government instituted a series of social reforms which diminished the role of the party, including freedom of the press and restrictions on the activities of the Czechoslovak secret police. Czechoslovakia also adopted a more independent foreign policy line by initiating diplomatic talks with the FRG.

While the Soviet leadership was primarily concerned about the direction of the "Prague Spring," the East Germans worried about the talks with the West Germans. Previously, the GDR had largely been successful in preventing such contacts by the other WTO states. Hard-liners in both countries, as well as in Poland, began to call for an intervention to end the reforms. The USSR attempted to pressure the Czechoslovak party leadership through WTO exercises in Czechoslovakia and in face-to-face meetings between the two party political bureaus.

Faced with allied pressures, concerns over possible contagion of the Czechoslovak reforms, and growing military anxieties, the USSR eventually decided to launch a military intervention to remove the Dubcek leadership. On August 20, 1968, units from five WTO states – Bulgaria, East Germany, Hungary, Poland, and the USSR – crossed into Czechoslovakia. The Czechoslovak government issued a non-resistance order and the intervention force quickly occupied the country.

Soviet troops made up the largest contingent of the 400,000-man intervention force, which was under Soviet, not WTO, command. The NVA's role in the intervention was largely "limited to preparatory activities" within East Germany, although some reconnaissance troops did enter Czechoslovakia.[29] Five Soviet divisions, two tank and three motor-rifle, remained in Czechoslovakia under a new command, the Central Group of Forces (CGF).[30] The stationing of these forces was governed by a treaty on the limited stay of Soviet troops.

The Soviets eventually managed to arrange a change in the government and the party, with Gustav Husak, Dubcek's replacement in the Slovak party, as the new First Secretary. While the Soviets moved to normalize relations with Czechoslovakia,[31] Brezhnev justified the intervention over concerns of counterrevolutionary behavior. In what would become known as the "Brezhnev Doctrine," he stated that socialist states had the right to intervene in another socialist state to protect the gains of socialism. In effect, the USSR placed limits on the freedom WTO states had in their domestic and foreign affairs.

In addition to limiting the sovereignty of socialist states, Brezhnev also warned the West that "the results of World War II are inviolable and we will defend them even at the cost of risking a new war."[32] Brezhnev was clearly defending the status quo in Eastern Europe and sought a return to alliance cohesion over viability. Other concerns would lead him to seek a more balanced approach, however.

DETENTE

By the late 1960s, the costs of the Cold War were beginning to increase for the USSR. The Soviet Army, for example, had recently begun an extensive modernization of their conventional forces. In addition, there was the threat of a new strategic arms race with the Americans over anti-ballistic missile defenses and a possible second front as the border tensions with China escalated to open conflict.

At the same time, the United States was bogged down in Vietnam and wanted Soviet assistance to end the conflict. These events led to the improvement in superpower relations in the early 1970s known as detente. Henry Kissinger, one of the architects of the American policies, viewed detente as a means to constrain Soviet behavior,[33] while the Soviets tended to see it as American confirmation of Soviet superpower status and recognition of the status quo in Europe.

Acceptance of the division of Europe allowed for an improvement in both inter-German and West German–Soviet relations. In 1969, the *Sozialdemokratische Partei Deutschlands* (SPD – Social Democratic Party of Germany) won the West German national elections for the first time. Willy Brandt, the new chancellor, sought to regularize contacts with the GDR and establish better relations with the USSR in what would become popularly known as *Ostpolitik* (east politics). Brezhnev was receptive to improved relations as a means of getting West German credits and technology.

In the GDR, however, Ulbricht was opposed to dealing with West Germany and to Brezhnev's *Westpolitik*. The Soviets engineered his removal as first secretary, although he did stay on as Chairman of the GDR Council of Ministers for a short period, and Erich Honecker was named the new head of the party. Honecker, who had been in charge of the construction of the Berlin Wall in 1961, accepted improved relations with the West. A series of agreements dealing with the status of Berlin, inter-German relations, the Polish border, and West German–Soviet relations were all signed in the early 1970s.

While detente between the superpowers proved short-lived over involvement in Third World conflicts, detente between the two Germanies would largely remain intact, subject to whatever limits the Soviets placed on the East Germans. Detente also signalled some improvement for the whole of Eastern Europe, as the Soviets allowed, and even encouraged, the East European states to borrow money from Western European banks to pay for improving the living standards of their people.

This East European consumerism was largely based on the Hungarian "New Social Contract." Following the Soviet invasion in 1956, the new leader of the HSWP, Janos Kadar, sought to establish some legitimacy by promising the

Hungarian people better living conditions in exchange for their acceptance of socialist rule. As part of this new contract, Hungary would later implement the New Economic Mechanism, which reintroduced some market mechanisms into the Hungarian economy. By the 1970s, most of the rest of WTO states would adopt consumerism as a means to increase their own legitimacy.

The East Germans, however, had introduced their own economic reforms in 1962, which sought to improve the efficiency of the socialist system. Consequently, the GDR never borrowed money from the West to the extent that many of the other countries in the region did, but then again the GDR was receiving financial assistance from the FRG in the form of direct payments. Detente, at least as it related to Eastern Europe, allowed the Soviets to reduce some of their financial supports for the non-Soviet WTO states. At the same time, however, the Soviets continued their conventional and strategic force modernization.

THE GSFG

As would follow with an elite force, the *Gruppa Sovetskikh Voisk v Germany* (Group of Soviet Forces in Germany) was one of the major recipients of this buildup. Throughout the 1970s and early 1980s, the GSFG would become an increasingly sophisticated and mechanized force. It, along with the NVA, with which it maintained "fraternal relations,"[34] formed the forward units of the first echelon of WTO forces and consequently was one of the most important Soviet commands, if not the most important.

The central role of the GSFG in Soviet defense plans can be gauged by the fact that it was commanded by a *glavnoko-mandyushchy* (commander-in-chief). Soviet Military Districts or Groups of Forces were more typically headed by a commander. This higher rank likely indicated that the GSFG command would have become the headquarters of the Western theater in the event of a war.[35] Somewhat less formally, many of the commanders of the forces in Germany went on to even higher positions in the Soviet Army, including two ministers of defense.[36]

As noted, the core of the GSFG was the wartime 1st Belorussian Front. Zhukov's command contained some of the most famous Soviet units from World War II, including the 8th Guards Army and the 1st and 2nd Guards Tank Armies. These units remained in Germany and were later reinforced by the 3rd *Udarnaya Armiya* (shock army) for breakthrough operations and the 20th Guards Army.[37] The 3rd Guards Tank Army, which had seen action in the war under Konyev's command, was withdrawn in the early 1960s.

The headquarters of the GSFG was located in the Berlin suburb of Zossen-Wunsdorf. In addition to having been the headquarters of the German *Oberkommand des Herres* (Supreme Command of the Army) during World War II and having excellent communication facilities, Zossen-Wunsdorf's proximity to West Berlin all but assured safety from a nuclear attack by the Western allies. The armies were located around major East German cities (see the map), with their forward units approximately eighty kilometers from the inner-German border.[38]

As with all Soviet units which were deployed outside the USSR, the units of the two motor-rifle and three tank armies were all Category A, which mean that they were maintained at at least eighty percent of their manpower and had all their allotted equipment.[39] In addition, all of the divisions in the Groups of Forces, which was the typical designation of Soviet commands outside the USSR, were also augmented with more tanks than those in the Soviet Military Districts.[40]

By the mid-1980s, the GSFG totalled nineteen motor-rifle and tank divisions, one artillery division, two surface-to-surface missile brigades, two surface-to-air missile brigades, an air assault brigade and a *spetsnaz* brigade. In addition, the ground forces were supported by an entire Air Army, designated as the Front Air Forces, GSFG.[41] In addition, at least one Operational Maneuver Group (OMG), also referred to as an Unified Army Corp, was created in the Western *Teatr Voyennikh Deystvy* (TVD – Theater of Military Operations) by combining a motor-rifle division with a tank division.[42]

GSFG Deployment

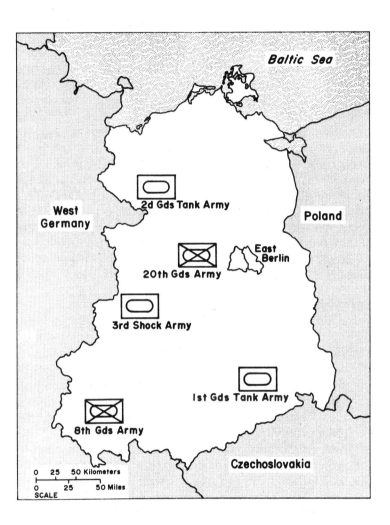

Sources: Central Intelligence Agency, *Atlas of Eastern Europe, August 1990* (Washington, DC: USGPO, 1990), 22; Erickson, Hansen and Schneider, *Soviet Ground Forces* (Boulder, Co: Westview, 1986), 38.

In terms of equipment, the GSFG fielded roughly 7,000 tanks (mainly the more modern T-72 and T-80 tanks), 2,350 infantry fighting vehicles, and 400 helicopters. The air force had about 1,200 aircraft. The total military personnel amounted to approximately 390,000, with almost 44,000 Soviet civilians assigned in a support capacity. The NVA added another six divisions, plus air and naval units, which amounted to another 160,000 soldiers.

· The GSFG and NVA represented the "sharp end of the stick" for any possible WTO attack against NATO. The forces in East Germany would have been supported by the Central and Northern Groups and Czech and Polish units. These forces accounted for the first echelon of the WTO and would be followed by a second echelon from the western military districts in the USSR. Such an operation would be under the command of the Soviet Western TVD and ultimately directed by the Soviet General Staff in Moscow.

THE DEEP BATTLE

Had NATO and the Warsaw Pact ever gone to war, the Soviets clearly wanted to fight as far west as possible and to win as quickly as possible. These desires were partly related to the Soviet experience in World War II when they were forced into a strategic defense, and partly reflected the greater American and Western European economic potential. Hence the Soviets wanted to knock out NATO and avoid a long war, which would have likely strained both the WTO alliance and the Soviet economy.

These concerns were reflected in Soviet military theory, with its emphasis on winning a war in the initial period, which was defined as the first stage of a war up to full mobilization by the combatants.[43] In the case of action against NATO, or any other adversary for that matter, the Soviets would have sought to:

> inflict a decisive defeat on the enemy's first strategic echelon; and then, by continuing with a speedy offensive into the depths of his territory, to complete his total defeat

before he was able to mobilise and make use of his military and economic potential.[44]

To be able to carry out this "decisive defeat" and "speedy offensive," the Soviets relied on what they termed *glubkaya operatsiya* (the deep operation).

The concept of the deep operation is largely credited to Marshal Mikhail Tukhachevsky, the Soviet Commissar of War in the mid-1930s, although his ideas were very much in line with Western theories of maneuver warfare of the 1920s and 1930s. The deep operation was conceptually similar to the German *blitzkrieg*, which relied on the insertion of mechanized forces through breeches in the enemy's lines in an attempt to disrupt the enemy's command and control. As in any form of maneuver warfare, it concentrated on movement and minimized combat. To put it simply, the offense attempts to outrun the defense.[45]

The GSFG, along with the NVA, would have likely attempted just such an attack had the Soviet leadership ever decided to go to war with NATO. Even with the post-war urban sprawl in northern Germany, the GSFG was in a better position to carry out such an operation than the other front-line unit, the Central Group in Czechoslovakia, because the CGF faced mountainous terrain. The other Groups of Forces in Hungary and Poland did not border NATO territory and could only act as reinforcements for the initial assault.[46]

Ideally, the GSFG would surprise the forces on NATO's Central Front and penetrate deeply into the FRG before NATO could adequately respond. NATO's defenses would then be disorganized since many of their units would be behind Soviet lines and the full weight of the Soviet attack would not be known. In addition, a deep penetration would mean that the Soviet units would be near West German civilians, precluding a NATO first use of nuclear weapons. As long as the Soviet units kept advancing, as stressed by Soviet doctrine, they should then reach the Rhine river, thereby splitting the Central Front.[47]

The Soviets did at least prepare for such a deep operation. As noted, the Soviet units tended to be more concentrated around their bases. In an attempt to be able to achieve the necessary surprise, GSFG units routinely charged the inner-German border. The Soviets also made extensive logistical preparations for such a strike. The Soviets built command and control facilities, as well as ammunition and fuel depots, throughout Eastern Europe, to manage and supply its deep attack. After the 1990 unification, for example, German officers discovered that the NVA had more ammunition than the much-larger West German *Bundeswehr*.[48]

Whether they would have succeeded is now, of course, a moot point. If the GSFG could have surprised NATO and if they had struck at a time when NATO was underprepared, say on a major holiday, then they may have very well been able to outrun NATO's forward defense.[49] From the Soviets' optimal point of view, such an operation would have been just one more river-to-river action, in this case from the Elbe to the Rhine, of the kind that they carried out so many times in World War II.

THE BURDENS OF ALLIANCE

As has been noted countless times, however, battles rarely go the way they were planned. Nor, for that matter, has there ever been any indication that the Soviets were actually going to attack NATO. The one thing that is certain is that the Soviets spent an enormous part of their budget to prepare for the possibility. By the 1980s, however, the Soviets were faced with increasing costs for their worldwide commitments.

As the Soviets modernized their forces, Western officials sought to counter Soviet capabilities through what were known as "competitive strategies." Given the Soviets' reliance on massed formations, NATO focused attention on sophisticated conventional weapons as a counter to the Soviets' advantages. Precision-guided munitions could be nearly as effective as tactical nuclear weapons in many situations. In combination with the American Strategic Defense Initiative, which would likely have had conventional applications as well, the increasing precision of modern weapons represented a qualitative increase in military technology, an increasingly expensive one that the Soviets would have to keep up with.

The WTO was also becoming more expensive, as the non-Soviet WTO armies were upgraded to a point that the "Northern Tier" militaries of Czechoslovakia, the GDR, and Poland, as well as Hungary's armed forces, were now close to Soviet standards. These states, however, were less willing to pay for this modernization[50] as their Western debts mounted. At the same time, consumerism began to lose its effectiveness in keeping Eastern Europe quiet. Soviet policies would come to a head when, in 1980, a strike in the shipyards of the Polish city of Gdansk led to the establishment of an independent trade union, Solidarity.

As with the Prague Spring, the Soviets wanted the Polish leadership to deal with this problem, but the party proved unable to come to terms with the Solidarity union. The Polish Minister of Defense, Wojciech Jaruzelski, took over as the First Secretary and declared martial law in December 1981. Even though the Soviets did not directly intervene, as in Hungary in 1956 and Czechoslovakia in 1968, the costs of the Polish martial law were still high, both internationally and in Eastern Europe.

The USSR was beginning to overextend itself, as its international commitments were becoming too expensive to maintain.[51] The security of the USSR, however, had always been a priority of the Soviet leadership and they had always been willing to pay the necessary costs in the past. Furthermore, control over Eastern Europe was a central component of this security after World War II. For the Soviets to give up their buffer zone, which was won at a cost of twenty-seven million dead, there had to be some change in their conception of national security.

3 The Beginnings of Disengagement

Suit the action to the word, the word to the action
  – William Shakespeare, *Hamlet*, Act III, scene ii

Historically, strategic overstretch has generally only been recognized after the fact. An intentional overextension would tend to run counter to any notion of rational behavior. In almost every other case of strategic overstretch, it took a major war to force a state to reduce its commitments. In the case of the USSR, however, it wasn't a global armed conflict but rather a change within the domestic political system that led the Soviet leadership to realize that they had overextended themselves in their Cold War against the United States.

That change was, of course, the ascension of Gorbachev to the position of General Secretary of the CPSU. Gorbachev's reforms would fundamentally change the USSR, although not entirely in the manner he intended. He also adopted a new style of foreign policy which sought to minimize international tensions related to the Cold War. It was the interplay between the domestic and foreign policy aspects of his reforms that would ultimately lead the USSR to begin to reduce its commitments and interests in Eastern Europe.

This chapter will look at Gorbachev, his reform effort, and how it affected Soviet foreign policy. Specifically, it will examine the reforms themselves, changes in Soviet policy towards the Third World and the West, and how Gorbachev came to deal with Eastern Europe.

THE RISE OF GORBACHEV

Mikhail Sergeevich Gorbachev was born in the North Caucasian village of Privolnoye in the Stavropol *krai*

39

(territory) in 1931. His background profoundly influenced his later career. For one thing, he reached adulthood under Stalin's rule, although he politically came of age in the Khrushchev and Brezhnev years. Both of his grandfathers were arrested in Stalin's purges, which seems to have made an impression upon him about the human costs of socialism. He was also too young to have served in the Red Army during World War II, although his village was briefly under German occupation in 1942.

While Stavropol is largely an agricultural region, Gorbachev went to and graduated from the law school at Moscow State University in 1955, returning to Stavropol to work in the *Komsomol*, the Communist youth organization, although he later switched to the party apparatus. It was in Stavropol that he met Fedor Kulakov, the first secretary of the party in the territory, who would become one of Gorbachev's principal mentors.

Gorbachev also had the opportunity to meet higher-ranking members of the CPSU in Stavropol. Both Mikhail Suslov, the Central Committee secretary in charge of ideology and widely held to be the person behind Khrushchev's ouster in 1964, and Yury Andropov, the chairman of the KGB, had ties to the North Caucasus and both vacationed in the region. Like Kulakov, they would also become Gorbachev supporters. When Kulakov, a rising star in Soviet politics in the 1970s, went to Moscow as the Central Committee secretary for agriculture, Gorbachev had three well-placed patrons in the CPSU *Politburo* (political bureau).

The North Caucasus has also had a history of freedom from Moscow. Serfdom was not practiced in the region, and, as a frontier area, it was always under somewhat looser control than much of the rest of the Tsarist Empire. These attitudes would continue even after the Soviets gained control over the region. Even though agriculture was collectivized in the 1930s, as it was throughout the USSR, the policy was never popular and farmers in the region implemented numerous experiments to increase output. Gorbachev seems to have adopted this more independent outlook, even in his university days.[1]

Gorbachev rose steadily, although not spectacularly, through the ranks, taking over Kulakov's old positions as his mentor advanced in the party. Had Kulakov not died under mysterious circumstances in 1978, the world might have never heard of Gorbachev, as he was merely one of many *kraikom* (territorial committee) party chairmen in the USSR. As it happened, he was selected to replace Kulakov as the CPSU Central Committee secretary in charge of agriculture and was made a candidate member of the *Politburo* in 1979. His ties with Andropov and Suslov apparently made the difference in securing his nomination.[2]

Upon his return to Moscow, Gorbachev was forty-eight years old, making him far and away the youngest member of Brezhnev's largely geriatric *Politburo*. One of Gorbachev's most important advantages in his later reform efforts was this beginning of a generational change in Soviet politics. Gorbachev's first years in the Secretariat and *Politburo* were relatively uneventful, although, following the American grain embargo in 1980, he sought to introduce an updated version of Lenin's New Economic Policy, which had originally attempted to reintroduce capitalism in the war-devastated economy in the 1920s.[3]

As the secretary in charge of agriculture, Gorbachev's political fortunes depended on agricultural output. After a particularly bad harvest in the fall of 1982, it was rumored that Brezhnev had decided to relieve Gorbachev, but put it off until after the November 7th celebrations. Brezhnev, however, never recovered from his attendance at the parade and died on November 10, 1982. Andropov, who had left the KGB in April 1982 to replace Suslov as the Second Secretary, was named General Secretary.[4]

Andropov, presumably well aware of the country's problems from his years as the head of the secret police, introduced some limited reforms to try to get the country moving again. Soon after taking office, however, he suffered kidney failure and had to be moved to a special clinic outside Moscow to receive dialysis treatment. While he was at the clinic, Gorbachev acted as his go-between with the rest of the

Politburo. Andropov would never be seen in public again and died in February 1984.

While Andropov was incapacitated, Gorbachev and the head of the Leningrad party organization, Georgy Romanov, were positioning themselves to succeed him. Gorbachev largely had the support of reformers, while Romanov had the backing of the more hard-line, military industrialists within the *Politburo*. Partly as a compromise, Konstantin Chernenko, a Brezhnev loyalist, was chosen as General Secretary but Gorbachev was named Second Secretary and purportedly was given a veto over Chernenko's actions.[5]

Like Andropov, Chernenko was in poor health, as he had emphysema, and was frequently out of sight. When Chernenko was too ill to attend, Gorbachev would chair the *Politburo* meetings. Unlike Andropov, Chernenko did not see any need for even limited reforms and actually ended Andropov's anti-corruption campaign. Chernenko lasted a little over a year in office and died on March 10, 1985. In a quickly convened meeting, Gorbachev was named General Secretary. At the time of his appointment, he was fifty-four years old, which made him the youngest General Secretary since Stalin.

THE REFORM EFFORT

Gorbachev's election marked a victory for the growing reform element within the CPSU. There was a general consensus within this group that Brezhnev had avoided too many decisions and that something had to change. Andropov's brief tenure only served to reinforce the sense of urgency. Gorbachev represented a second chance to change the still-largely Stalinist system before it was too late and the USSR went into an irreversible decline.

Like Andropov and Chernenko, Gorbachev stressed continuity with the policies of his predecessor. Indeed, if one looked at his political career, there was little reason to believe e would support radical change. His first major attempt to overhaul Soviet society was the abortive anti-alcohol campaign. Soviet alcoholic consumption was one of the highest in the world and negatively affected, among other things, birth rates, health, and production. Gorbachev introduced measures to limit alcohol production and sales and develop alternative pastimes. The anti-alcohol plan backfired, however, as it reduced also state revenues from the sales of alcohol.[6]

What was needed was something more systemic. Although Gorbachev initially couched his proposals in Marxist-Leninist language, calling for the country "to accelerate the socioeconomic development of society,"[7] he would eventually move to reduce the authority and role of the centralized command system that dominated Soviet society. Gorbachev's first major statement of the coming changes was in his report to the 27th Party Congress of the CPSU in February 1986.

In his speech, Gorbachev noted that "in the 1970s, difficulties began to mount up in the national economy."[8] The principal reason for these difficulties was the lack of "timely political evaluations of the change in the economic situation."[9] As noted, this "period of stagnation," a reference to the later Brezhnev years, had brought the USSR to a state of "pre-crisis."[10] Gorbachev sought to remedy these problems by introducing a "new quality of growth,"[11] or expansion of intensive growth, into the Soviet economy and increasing popular participation.

These new changes would be brought about by his reforms of *glasnost*, *demokratizatsiya*, and *perestroika*. To Gorbachev, the most important component of his reforms was the restructuring of the Soviet economy, although public participation, through the increase of social freedoms, was to be the guarantor of the economic and political changes. In short, Gorbachev wanted to introduce personal initiative and responsibility into a command system. A more Western-oriented focus on the individual was to be developed in the collectivist system of state socialism.

While his reforms ultimately proved somewhat contradictory, as Gorbachev thought he could control the process of reform, *glasnost* and *demokratizatsiya* did bring about a fundamental change in Soviet society. By opening up the system, groups within and outside the party began to call for even more fundamental and radical changes. As the government was reorganized along more democratic lines, these groups then won representation in legislative bodies, giving them an official platform for their reform efforts.

In addition, by calling for "stating the truth,"[12] Gorbachev brought about a fundamental questioning of the system. More and more of the Soviet past beyond the "period of stagnation" was open to criticism. This process led to Gorbachev's promise that there would be "no forgotten names or blank spots" in Soviet history, which ultimately meant dealing with the Stalin period. A special commission was convened to investigate Stalin's purges and several prominent Bolsheviks were rehabilitated.[13] Although Gorbachev was careful to blame Stalin personally for the expansion of the command system into the social and political spheres of society, these new criticisms largely undermined the Soviet system.

In an attempt to deal with the social forces unleashed by his reforms, Gorbachev introduced measures that sought to remove the excesses of the system but still keep things under control. In agriculture, for example, although he continued with the largely failed system of collectivized farming, Gorbachev also introduced the concept of lease-holding, which would have allowed farmers to work a specific plot of land in perpetuity. He never moved to allow private ownership of the land. In other areas of the economy, he would call for "diverse forms of ownership," which ultimately included a plan for the transition to a market economy.[14]

Gorbachev, following in a long line of Russian and later Soviet reformers, sought a revolution from above. But unlike the other reformers, he also wanted to pressure the centralized system from below to prevent a counteraction against him as had happened to Khrushchev. In both cases, he wanted to bring Soviet practices somewhat more in line with Western ideals, to reintegrate the USSR with the world. This process also implied a change in Soviet foreign policy.

NEW POLITICAL THINKING

Gorbachev's reform process was also applied to international relations, where he sought to reduce the role of ideology in Soviet foreign policy and to bring Soviet interests more in line with changes in the late twentieth-century world. The foreign component of his reforms was known as *novoe politicheskoe myshlenie*, or new political thinking. This new thinking was clearly linked to his domestic reforms in that it represented the extension of *glasnost* and *perestroika* to foreign issues.

The fundamental change of the new political thinking was the deideologization of foreign policy. Concerns other than class interests, such as environmental problems, growing economic interdependence, and the threat of nuclear weapons, were now recognized as valid and possibly more important than the promotion of socialism throughout the world. Universal values would also determine Soviet interests, not simply proletarian internationalism. Consequently, the Cold War could be allowed to recede to some degree, while assistance to "countries of socialist orientation" could be diminished.

The reduction in ideology did not mean that Gorbachev was ready to abandon the WTO states. Rather, relations with Eastern Europe were at the heart of his reforms since Eastern Europe was expected to contribute to Soviet restructuring through "mutually beneficial economic ties," which would entail "a transition in the economic relations between them from mainly trade links to deeper specialization and cooperation in production."[15] It would also mean that the communist regimes in Eastern Europe would have to be viable partners, becoming real allies and not simply Soviet "puppets."

New thinking also called for a re-examination of Soviet security, including "the nature of the Western threat."[16] Gorbachev would eventually question the traditional Soviet concern with absolute security. Since new thinking placed common concerns above class interests, the West did not, therefore, represent as much of a threat to the USSR as it had before. Consequently, Soviet military expenditures could be reduced, which would allow for the reallocation of resources to aid the economic restructuring, while agreements with the West could reduce military forces on both sides, potentially enhancing Soviet security.

The changes in foreign policy also sought to integrate the USSR into the world economy, while the domestic reforms would allow for greater Western participation in the Soviet economy. Unlike detente, however, Western assistance was not seen as a panacea and greater emphasis was initially placed on domestic solutions. The most important foreign contribution to the reforms would be the reduction of international tensions, which would allow the Soviets to deal with their problems.

In all of the facets of new thinking, Gorbachev was clearly trying to reduce Soviet foreign commitments to pay for his socialist renewal. New political thinking, as with the domestic reforms, did not represent an abandonment of socialism, nor was it a permanent solution to the existence of two social systems, capitalism and socialism. Rather, it sought to promote common interests and minimize, if not prevent, conflict while the Soviets got their act together.

AFGHANISTAN

One of the most pressing foreign policy problems Gorbachev inherited was the war in Afghanistan. Since 1979, Soviet soldiers had been fighting opponents of the communist government of the country, with few signs of success. Many countries, including the United States and Britain, openly supplied weapons to the rebel forces. Diplomatic efforts, through the United Nations (UN), had been unsuccessful as well. In a very real sense, Afghanistan was the first foreign policy test of Gorbachev's reforms.

The Afghan conflict was largely Brezhnev's war. While the Soviets had been providing aid to Afghanistan since 1955, it was Brezhnev who expanded the contacts between the Soviets and the Afghans, especially with the Afghan communists, the People's Democratic Party of Afghanistan (PDPA). In the mid-1970s, the USSR supported the leftist regime of Daoud Khan with large-scale economic assistance and continued this support when Daoud was overthrown by pro-Soviet Afghan Army officers in 1978. The PDPA established a People's Republic and introduced widespread economic and political reforms.

These secular reforms, however, led to armed opposition within the deeply religious Moslem country. The government responded with military attacks against rebel villages, which only led to increased opposition and, by late 1978, Afghanistan was in a civil war. The rebels were supported by Pakistan's intelligence agency, while the Afghan government relied more and more on the USSR. The Soviets provided advisors, economic aid, and weapons to help the PDPA put down the rebellion. Soviet assistance proved ineffective, however, and the Afghan government's hold on the country weakened.

Faced with the potential loss of an ally, one that Brezhnev had elevated to the same ideological status as the USSR or the WTO states, the Soviets opted to intervene militarily. On December 24, 1979, Soviet airborne troops were airlifted into the country, while KGB special units overthrew the head of the country, Hafizullah Amin, in a raid and Babrak Karmal was installed as the new President. Three days later, two Soviet motor-rifle divisions crossed into Afghanistan. The Brezhnev Doctrine had been invoked once again.

Unlike in Czechoslovakia in 1968, however, the population did not acquiesce to the intervention. The introduction of Soviet troops only led to more opposition and many Afghan Army troops defected to the rebels. Karmal had virtually no legitimacy, since it was widely held that he "rode into power on a Soviet tank,"[17] and the government's authority extended only as far as there were Soviet troops present. The initial show of force failed to produce support for the government.

The Soviets then turned to military operations to physically defeat the rebels. In the spring of 1980, the 40th Army, the Soviet command in Afghanistan, began a series of offensives against the insurgents. These attacks largely followed Soviet conventional doctrine, complete with detailed objectives. The rebels would simply withdraw in the face of such assaults and re-occupied the territory after the Soviets went back to their bases. In between the offensives, Soviet convoys were subjected to hit-and-run attacks by the rebels. The Soviets' initial response to the ineffectiveness of the "pacification sweeps," as the offensives were known, was to increase the scale of the attacks.

The larger offensives only led to more Soviet casualties and by 1985 the Soviets switched to special forces to take the war to the rebels. Soon after taking power, however, Gorbachev appears to have decided that the Afghan intervention simply wasn't worth it and that the USSR needed to get out.[18] By 1986, aside from the special units, Soviet troops were largely restricted to garrison duties as much of the fighting was turned over to the Afghan government. More importantly, Gorbachev began to look for a way out. Negotiations under UN auspices were intensified to get an international agreement while the Soviets pressured the PDPA to share power.

These two aspects of Soviet policy represented new thinking as it would be applied to Third World conflicts. The Soviets sought to disengage themselves from the military aspect of the conflict, while trying to get their ally to improve their legitimacy by entering into negotiations with the opposition forces. In the case of Afghanistan, the Soviets pressured Karmal to resign in 1986 and promoted Sayid Mohammed Najibullah, the head of the Afghan secret police, as his successor. Najibullah introduced Afghan versions of Gorbachev's domestic reforms and attempted to bring moderate rebel groups into his government through his policy of national reconciliation.

Part of national reconciliation involved the reduction of the Soviet military presence. As noted, Gorbachev eventually limited Soviet ground actions to the special forces, although air units still supported Afghan Army operations. The major breakthrough in the conflict, however, was the UN-sponsored Geneva Accords signed in March 1988 which called for the Soviets to withdraw over a nine-month period. The Soviets, who also acted as one of the guarantors of the accords, began to pull out in May and completed their withdrawal in February 1989, a day ahead of schedule.

Although the struggle between the PDPA and the rebels continued until 1992, and although the USSR and the United States continued for a time to supply their respective sides, the war was now largely an internal Afghan affair. Some of the Afghan rebels, who were now no longer fighting a foreign power, entered into agreements with the Najibullah government. The de-escalation of the Afghan conflict was largely the result of new thinking, as well as evidence of the fundamental change it represented.

PROXY WARS

Afghanistan was only one of several Soviet Third World allies that faced an insurgency by pro-Western rebels. The difference between Afgahnistan and these other countries was that Soviet troops actually fought in Afghanistan, while the other conflicts, also known as pro-insurgencies, became proxy wars between the United States and the USSR. The United States, acting under the so-called Reagan Doctrine, supplied these various anti-communist rebels as a means of raising the costs of the Soviets' involvement in the Third World. For their part, the Soviets supported their embattled ideological allies, largely without any economic or strategic considerations.

As in Afghanistan, the expansion of Soviet commitments to many of these socialist-leaning countries occurred under the Brezhnev regime. The Soviets had originally supported pro-Soviet factions in several Third World struggles. When these factions won out over their rivals and took control of the government, they introduced the Soviet system of centralized control despite the inapplicability or the feasibility of such a system for a Third World country. They also adopted many Soviet political practices, including a one-party state, supported by a secret police, and tight control of the military.

It was largely the repressive policies of these Soviet allies that led to the rebellions, although the Western countries did step in to provide aid and training. The pro-insurgencies only served to further weaken the Soviet allies, as they now had to spend their resources fighting a rebellion. In turn, the Soviets had to then increase their financial and military support for these countries. In addition to the economic drain, these conflicts also tended to point out the bankruptcy of socialism as a model for other Third World states.[19]

As with Afghanistan, Gorbachev seems to have decided early on that the USSR needed to disengage from these conflicts. Just like the PDPA, the ruling parties would have to stand on their own, as Soviet support was largely reduced or, in some cases, withdrawn. *Perestroika* required that resources be spent more carefully, while continued Soviet involvement in Third World conflicts tended to contradict *glasnost* and new thinking.

In some cases, such as Mozambique, where the government was fighting the South-African-backed *Renamo* movement, Soviet aid was quickly reduced. Around the same time, the Mozambique leadership had begun to question the viability of socialism and introduced political and economic reforms allowing for multiple parties and a free market economy. Other states would continue to receive aid but, by the end of the 1980s, Soviet assistance was beginning to subside as the Soviets sought other means to resolve the conflicts.

In the case of Angola, the USSR entered into UN-sponsored negotiations to try to solve the civil war between the Angolan government and UNITA, the rebel movement. Soviet support, which included logistical support for the Cuban troops in Angola, was eventually reduced after Western aid to the rebels was reduced. The Soviet reduction of aid ultimately included the withdrawal of the Cuban forces. As in Afghanistan and Mozambique, the ruling MPLA would introduce reforms, which culminated in the 1993 elections in the country, although the rebels initially refused to accept the MPLA victory.

Soviet aid to Ethiopia would follow much the same pattern as Mozambique and Angola and largely had the same consequences. The Soviets eventually decided to reduce their support for Ethiopia's war against Ethiopian rebels and Eritrean separatists. When the aid was eventually cut off, the government's military position quickly disintegrated and the

Ethiopian rebels captured Addis Ababa in 1992, promising free elections and allowing the province of Eritrea to secede.

The most-publicized of these proxy wars, however, was the struggle between the socialist Sandinista government of Nicaragua and the American-backed Contras. Although the Sandinistas came to power through their own insurgency, the Soviets and the Cubans quickly provided support for the leftist regime. When the nature of their policies became evident, former Nicaraguan National Guard personnel, known as the Contras, began their own rebellion, which was just as quickly supported by Washington. The United States was also concerned over Nicaraguan support of Marxist guerrillas in El Salvador.

Gorbachev actually increased assistance to Nicaragua at first, as the Contras had received increased support from the United States and were putting severe pressure on the government.[20] The general pattern of Soviet disengagement would later take hold, however, as the West called for Moscow to pressure the Sandinistas to accept a compromise agreement. The Soviets got the government to agree to hold elections, which resulted in the surprise victory of the opposition party, although some Sandinistas initially remained in the government.[21]

Although many of these proxy wars were not finally resolved, if at all, until after the events of 1989 in Eastern Europe, it was in the Third World that Gorbachev began the process of dealing with the overextended strategic position he had largely inherited from Brezhnev. Soviet commitments in the Third World were clearly secondary and blatantly counterproductive for the Soviets, which made it that much easier for Gorbachev to change policies. New thinking, however, was soon to be applied to a more central problem.

EURO-STRATEGIC CONCERNS

Brezhnev, it will be remembered, not only expanded Soviet interests in the Third World, but also built up the Soviet Army's conventional and nuclear capabilities. His successors, including Gorbachev, would continue to modernize the Soviet military in an attempt to keep up or catch the West technologically. Gorbachev, however, also sought to reduce the threat from NATO, which would have the effect of easing the Soviet modernization burden. The initial Soviet effort at European threat reduction dealt primarily with theater nuclear weapons, but also on preventing a new anti-ballistic missile defense.

In the mid-1970s, the USSR deployed an intermediate range ballistic missile (IRBM), designated the RSD-10 *Pioner* (Pioneer), and known in the West as the SS-20. Essentially two stages of an intercontinental ballistic missile, the RSD-10 represented a significant upgrading of Soviet theater capabilities. Instead of relying on older SS-4 and SS-5 IRBMs located in the republics of Belorussia and the Ukraine to target NATO forces, the RSD-10 could hit Western Europe from bases in the expanses of Siberia. The range of the RSD-10, approximately 4,000 kilometers, was such that, along with the Soviet "Backfire" bomber, it could be considered an "Eurostrategic" weapon.[22]

The deployment of the RSD-10, much like Soviet involvement in the Third World, proved to be counterproductive, however. NATO moved against this new threat by deploying two American theater weapons, the Pershing II, a medium range ballistic missile and "Tomahawk" ground launched cruise missiles (GLCM) in sites in Holland, Italy, and West Germany. The Pershing IIs were capable of reaching the western USSR in about eight minutes, while the GLCMs would be able to fly under Soviet radar, making detection difficult. The NATO deployment, therefore, represented a direct threat against the Soviet command and control network.[23]

Shortly after the NATO deployment, the United States began research into the development of a Strategic Defense Initiative (SDI), popularly known as "Star Wars." This move represented a double-edged sword to the USSR. On one hand, if SDI was successful, the USSR would lose its second strike capability to retaliate against an American first strike. On the other hand, as noted, the Soviets were also concerned about potential conventional spin-offs of SDI. The Soviets' initial response to both American programs was negative and they sought to counter both largely through public relations campaigns in the West.

The Soviets also adopted their own countermeasure to the NATO theater nuclear forces. They moved more modern short-range nuclear launchers, SS-21s and SS-23s, into East Germany and Czechoslovakia. These Soviet tactical deployments were clearly forced on the two allies. Gorbachev largely continued with the Soviet response to both SDI and the American theater forces at first, although the USSR announced an unilateral moratorium on nuclear testing in 1985.

A major catalyst in changing Gorbachev's thinking about nuclear weapons seems to have been the accident at the Soviet nuclear power plant at Chernobyl on April 25, 1986. Even though it was the worst nuclear reactor accident in history, the potential for a catastrophe was far greater. In addition, the enormous expense of the cleanup would cut into the funds available for *perestroika* and it also demonstrated that the USSR needed Western assistance to deal with the accident.[24] That fall, when Gorbachev met with Ronald Reagan, the American president, in Reykjavik, Iceland, he proposed sweeping reductions in both sides' nuclear arsenals.

Although Gorbachev's Reykjavik proposals ultimately foundered on the issue of SDI, they did serve notice that Gorbachev was willing to deal on the issue of the theater or, as it would become known, intermediate-range nuclear forces (INF). In February 1987, Gorbachev dropped the linkage between the reduction of INF and the elimination of SDI, which led to the INF talks between the United States and the USSR.

The negotiations culminated in the INF Treaty, which was signed in Washington, DC on December 8, 1987. It was the first arms control treaty to eliminate two classes, both intermediate and shorter-range, of nuclear weapons launchers. Soviet and American nuclear weapons, totaling about 2,600 warheads with a range of 500–5,500 kilometers, were to be destroyed. Hence the Soviets could not simply redeploy the

RSD-10s in the eastern part of Siberia, which was a major American concern. The treaty also called for on-site inspections to verify the treaty, which was the first time the Soviets ever agreed to an "intrusive" verification system.

The INF Treaty pointed to significantly improved superpower relations, although it did not lead to immediate breakthroughs in either strategic or conventional arms talks. Nevertheless, it represented evidence that the Soviets were now willing to admit that their past behavior had been counterproductive as they openly acknowledged that it was their deployments that led to the NATO counter-deployments. More importantly, they were now willing to cut their losses and negotiate.

In both relations with the Third World and the United States, Gorbachev clearly placed greater emphasis on a cost–benefit analysis than previous General-Secretaries. If a past policy had not provided ample return on the resources invested, then he proved quite willing to change. As the Soviet economy failed to respond to his reforms, however, this cost–benefit analysis was applied to even more central policies.

DEFENSE ISSUES

One of the most controversial aspects of *perestroika* was military reform. By the late 1980s, the Soviets were undergoing the most extensive review of national security policy since the early days of the Bolshevik regime.[25] Gorbachev would eventually recognize that the previous Soviet policy of seeking absolute security only engendered new threats, as other countries felt threatened by the Soviet buildup. At the same time, Gorbachev needed to reduce the military's share of the budget to pay for his restructuring.

This reform involved many changes in Soviet defense policy, all of which related to Gorbachev's stated policy of *razumnaya dostatochnost*, or reasonable sufficiency. Reasonable sufficiency, also referred to as defensive sufficiency or reasonable sufficiency for defense, was first publicly stated, but not at length, by Gorbachev during a state visit to France in 1985. Basically, reasonable sufficiency involved restructuring the Soviet Army to carry out a successful defense. In theory, the offensive orientation of the military would be dropped, as units would be reconfigured for defensive operations and the military reduced in size.

Reasonable sufficiency, however, was interpreted in many different ways. Western analysts minimized the stated doctrinal changes, as the Soviets had always stressed the defensive orientation of the Soviet Army. More important, there were debates within the Soviet military as to what constituted reasonable sufficiency. Dmitry Yazov, the Soviet defense minister since 1987, tended to view it as allowing for an offensive phase after a successful defense, while others, including civilian defense experts, stressed the defensive aspect.

These debates pointed out the changes within the Soviet defense establishment, as the military's control over national security policy was weakened by Gorbachev. Doctrinal changes weren't the only reform, although they were the central ones. Gorbachev's social reforms were also applied to the military. The Soviet minister of finance, for example, released more accurate figures for the defense budget than in the past, while Soviet space launches, which were under the control of the military, were broadcast live. The Soviet press began to publish more accurate accounts of the fighting in Afghanistan as well.

Older Brezhnev appointees were retired by Gorbachev and replaced with largely younger, better educated officers, who tended to agree with the goals of *perestroika*, if not *glasnost*. The military seemed to have initially accepted the reforms as a means to prevent them from losing ground technologically. Gorbachev did continue with the planned modernization of both the conventional and nuclear forces throughout his tenure.[26] He, as had his predecessors, stressed maintaining a strong military. The difference was in relation to what.

Gorbachev would eventually propose "a new model of security," one that involved a cooperative "reduction of armaments."[27] This new compromise model would take into account the legitimate defensive needs of states, but also non-military concerns such as environmental problems as well as the threat of nuclear weapons. To promote this new defensive thinking, Gorbachev announced an unilateral reduction of the Soviet armed forces during his 1988 UN speech.

He stated that he would reduce the Soviet Army by 500,000 men, or 10 percent of the armed forces, over the next two years, with significant reductions in the Soviet forces in Eastern Europe. The USSR planned, in agreement with its WTO allies, to withdraw six tank divisions from Czechoslovakia, the GDR, and Hungary by 1991. These divisions were to be disbanded and not redeployed to the USSR. The Soviets would also withdraw air assault and assault engineer units, along with assault-crossing equipment, including bridging equipment, from Eastern Europe. These reductions would amount to 50,000 men and 5,000 tanks.[28]

Units in the European USSR would also be reduced by approximately the same amount. In addition, the units that remained in the Groups of Forces would be reorganized along more defensive lines. The number of tanks within the motor-rifle divisions was cut from 260 to 155, a 40 percent reduction, while the tank component of the tank divisions was reduced from 320 to 250, a 20 percent cut.[29] These reductions would, according to Gorbachev, allow for the maintenance of a "reasonable and dependable sufficiency, so that no one is tempted to encroach upon the security of the USSR or its allies."[30]

It was also intended to reduce the possibility of a war between NATO and the WTO.[31] Many of the other states of the WTO also reduced their armed forces (see Table 1). East Germany, for example, followed the Soviet lead and announced a 10 percent cut in its armed forces in 1989. These reductions were not necessarily seen as weakening the pact's defense capabilities.[32] In addition, WTO exercises now focused more on defensive operations.[33] At the same time, Gorbachev announced that Soviet units in Outer Mongolia would also be withdrawn. He had clearly put the Soviet Army on the defensive, in more ways than one.

Table 1   Eastern European Announced Force Reductions

	Bulgaria	CSSR	GDR	Hungary	Poland
Troops	10,000	12,000	10,000	9,300	40,000
Tanks	200	850	600	251	850
Guns	200	–	–	430	400
Aircraft	20	51	50	9	80
Armoured Vehicles	–	150	–	30	700

Source: *Soviet Military Power, 1989*, op. cit., p. 62.

RELATIONS WITH EASTERN EUROPE

When Gorbachev came to office in 1985, Eastern Europe was largely still reeling from the events of the early 1980s: the imposition of martial law in Poland; the NATO INF deployment; a worsening economic picture for the region; and the death of Brezhnev, a general secretary many of the Eastern European leaders could identify with. Gorbachev, on the other hand, represented an unknown quantity for the rest of the WTO.

At first, Gorbachev largely followed Soviet practices in dealing with Eastern Europe, although he devoted a great deal of attention to the region, holding six Pact summits in his first year. Generally, he sought to improve the existing structures and institutions of both CEMA and the WTO.[34] As noted, Eastern Europe was to play a role in Soviet economic reform, by creating joint ventures with Soviet companies and through increased economic cooperation as called for by the Comprehensive Program of CEMA.[35]

By and large, Gorbachev's policies towards the region met with the approval of the Eastern European leaders, once they realized that Gorbachev was not planning on retiring them any time soon.[36] Honecker, whose 1984 trip to West Germany had been vetoed by the Soviets over the INF issue, was especially relieved that ties between the two Germanies could continue. Just as with his initial domestic and other foreign policies, Gorbachev had not given any indication of radical changes.

But as Gorbachev introduced more systemic reforms in the USSR, his position on Eastern Europe changed as well. The USSR could no longer afford to maintain hegemony over the region. While the USSR was restructuring itself, Eastern Europe was going to be on its own.[37] Although the Soviets would clearly have preferred the other WTO states to introduce similar reforms, only Hungary and Poland did so. Most of the rest of the countries preferred to maintain the status quo.

Gorbachev began his reform process with the intention of saving socialism, both in the USSR and in Eastern Europe. He recognized that Stalin's version of socialism could not work and sought to remove these "accretions" from Soviet society. In terms of Eastern Europe, this process meant that each state had to develop along their own path, that there was not one single socialist model for all to follow. Gorbachev noted that no one country had:

> the right to claim special status in the socialist world. We consider the independence of every party, its responsibility to the people of its own country, and its right to decide the questions of the country's development to be unconditional principles.[38]

In other words, Gorbachev decided, once and for all, in favor of the viability of the WTO states over pact cohesion.

Gorbachev also resurrected, although in a significantly altered version, Brezhnev's concept of *Obshcheevropeisky Dom*, or a "Common European Home." Proposed during his 1987 visit to Czechoslovakia, the "Common European Home" was based on "a degree of integrity" in Europe, based on the shared cultural–historical background.[39] Gorbachev called for European states to cooperate towards finding solutions to common problems, especially those relating to security issues. Europe, according to this view, should "not be a citadel with embrasures, powder magazines and missile

ences, but a peaceful home without weapons."[40] Just as new
thinking sought to reintegrate the USSR with the rest of the
world, the Common European Home was largely an attempt
to reconcile eastern and western Europe.

The results of Gorbachev's new thinking towards Eastern
Europe were somewhat paradoxical. Many of the leaders,
most of whom had been in power long before Gorbachev, had
little interest in pursuing Gorbachev-style reforms. On the
other hand, Gorbachev became a symbol of change for many
reformers in the region and they would look increasingly
towards the USSR for inspiration and hope. To complicate
matters, the idea of the "Common European Home,"
increased the possibilities of renewed historical ties with the
West.

Gorbachev did not quite anticipate the magnitude of the
changes that were to come, nor did he completely live up to his
own words. In the fall of 1987, he engineered the removal of
Husak as First Secretary of the Czechoslovak party. Milos
Jakes, hardly a reformer, was named as Husak's successor.
Gorbachev would later attempt to pressure the more hard-line
leaders, including Honecker, to accept the now inevitable need
for changes, but by 1989, it was largely too late.

The principal reason for the coming collapse of socialism in
Eastern Europe was Gorbachev's renunciation of the Brezhnev Doctrine. Throughout the later 1980s, the Soviets stressed
acceptance of Eastern European autonomy, diversity and even
plurality,[41] all of which pointed towards a reluctance to
intervene as they had in Hungary or Czechoslovakia. The one
thing Gorbachev did stress was that the states of Eastern
Europe should acknowledge their treaty obligations, above all
their security ties, but other Soviet officials hinted that the
USSR would eventually accept Hungarian neutrality.

The coming Soviet withdrawal from Afghanistan, the
announced unilateral Soviet arms reductions, and suggestions
about a long-term, total withdrawal from Eastern Europe
forced the issue, however, and in a joint declaration issued
during his March 1988 visit to Yugoslavia, Gorbachev
publicly repudiated the notion of limited sovereignty for
socialist states. The following year, Gennady Gerasimov, a

Soviet Ministry of Foreign Affairs spokesman, would declare
that the Brezhnev doctrine had been replaced by the "Sinatra
Doctrine," because the Eastern Europe was "doing it their
way."[42]

Gorbachev had come almost full circle in regards to Eastern
Europe. When he took over, he largely continued Brezhnev's
policies, but by the end of the decade, he had accepted the end
of Soviet control over the region. By accepting pluralism, he
also had to accept the end of socialism in the region, the very
thing he wanted to avoid. While this process could be
considered largely one of improvisation,[43] it was still a
testament to new political thinking and Gorbachev's will
ingness to accept change.

THE CONSEQUENCES OF NEW THINKING

In seeking a socialist renewal, Gorbachev's reforms led to a
systemic crisis for both Eastern Europe and the USSR. New
political thinking, like *glasnost*, *demokratizatsiya*, and *perestroika* in the USSR, had unleashed nationalist and societal
forces in the WTO states that were beyond anyone's control
Gorbachev's policy revolution of allowing for the possibility
of genuine reform unintentionally made it probable, as
Eastern Europe reformers sought to move away from the
USSR, to go "back to Europe."[44]

Above all, it was the reconceptualization of Soviet national
security that would lead to the events of 1989. The beginnings
of a Soviet withdrawal, as part of Gorbachev's force
reductions, and the renunciation of the right to intervene
gave nationalist reformers in Eastern Europe a limited green
light. The combination of the changes in Soviet policy towards
Eastern Europe and in security matters would also lead to a
questioning of the central component of Soviet post-war
foreign policy, namely a weak Germany.

4 The East German Revolution

To be or not to be – that is the question
  – William Shakespeare, *Hamlet*, Act III, scene i

The communist leaders of the non-Soviet WTO states each reacted quite differently to Gorbachev's reforms, yet they were all replaced by pro-reform leaders by the end of 1989. Throughout the year, reformers in Eastern Europe would test the limits of acceptable change, discovering an ally for change in the USSR in the process, and finding that the hard-line communists were largely unable or unwilling to act against organized opposition. Even more quickly than it had been established after World War II, state socialism in Eastern Europe fell, almost literally like dominoes.

East Germany was not isolated from these events, and indeed, underwent what was probably the most dramatic revolution of the year, which culminated in the destruction of the Berlin Wall. As in all of the revolutions, East Germany's was due to a multitude of factors, but even more so than the others, it largely occurred due to the new Soviet policy of leaving the socialist regimes to fend for themselves. The USSR not only acquiesced to a change in the leadership of the East German government but even encouraged it.

This chapter, then, will examine the development of political pluralism in East Germany, as well as in other countries in the region, the 1989 revolution, the establishment of a new government, and Soviet actions and reactions to these events.

HUNGARIAN AND POLISH INTERLUDES

The East German revolution might never had happened if Hungarian and Polish reformers had not attempted earlier, although somewhat more incremental, changes in their countries. Not only did they represent the possibility of achieving systemic reform of the Soviet-style command system, but events in Hungary would also play a more direct role in the coming confrontation between East German hard-liners and reformers.

As noted, Hungary and Poland were the only non-Soviet WTO states that embraced Gorbachev's reforms. The leaders of both countries saw *glasnost* and *perestroika* as allowing them a means to achieve greater legitimacy at a time when they desperately needed it. By 1987, Kadar had entered his fourth decade of rule, while the economic reforms were losing steam. Hungary was running a trade deficit, as its products were not competitive on the world market, and suffered from sagging agricultural prices and a lack of innovation. An expansion of the economic reforms, combined with increased social reforms, might therefore renew Kadar's social contract.

In Poland, Jaruzelski had to deal with a deteriorating economy and a breakdown between society and the government. Despite its continued outlaw status, Solidarity still existed as an underground movement. In addition, the Roman Catholic Church served as a sort of "loyal opposition" to the government and had close ties to Solidarity. At the same time, the Polish economy had only slightly recovered from the near-collapse of the early eighties. Here too, Gorbachev-style reforms might help maintain the socialist system and prevent another crisis like the one in 1980–81.

Like Gorbachev, however, both Kadar and Jaruzelski would find out that it is one thing to introduce limited decentralization and quite another to control this new independence. In Kadar's case, the reforms would eventually overtake him and he was removed as First Secretary in May 1988, although he continued as the largely-ceremonial President. He was replaced by Karoly Grosz, who, like Gorbachev, was in favor of limited reforms, especially economic reform.[1]

Despite his reputation as being the "Hungarian Ligachev," after the hard-line CPSU ideology secretary, Yegor Ligachev, Grosz would eventually preside over the dismantling of the HSWP and communist rule. With Gorbachev's approval,

Grosz purged Kadar's associates from the HSWP *Politburo* and replaced them with reformers. He also moved Hungary towards a market economy, reducing state control even further. Most importantly, Grosz, under pressure from the reformers he had elevated to the *Politburo* and also from opposition leaders, began to accept the need for some sort of "institutionalized power-sharing" with opposition forces.

In November 1988, the Hungarian Smallholders Party, a conservative agrarian party which had been active in Hungarian politics prior to the imposition of a one-party system, was recognized as a legal party. Although their electoral support was limited, this recognition broke the monopoly of the HSWP and was quickly followed by the legalization of other opposition parties. By allowing a multiparty system, the communists accepted the loss of their special status in society. Instead of playing the leading role in society, they were now reduced to being "the prime negotiator."[2]

The HSWP also had to accept playing by the rules it had established. They recognized independent opposition organizations, such as the Hungarian Democratic Forum or the Alliance of Free Democrats, both of which would become major Hungarian political parties. Both groups served as umbrella organizations for other, smaller opposition movements or forces.[3] They were two of the major participants of the Hungarian Round Table negotiations with the government on the transition to a more pluralistic system.

In Poland, labor unrest in the fall of 1988 would lead to similar talks, also known as the Round Table, between the government and Solidarity, although in this case, Jaruzelski consulted with Gorbachev prior to entering into these discussions. The government wanted Solidarity's help in ending a strike by coal miners in Silesia, which was crippling the Polish economy, while the nominally illegal union wanted reinstatement as a recognized body. They would eventually come to terms, which included a two-year moratorium on strikes in the country, recognition of Solidarity, and the establishment of a new upper house, the Senate, in the Polish legislature and also the office of president.

This agreement also called for the first semi-free elections in Eastern Europe since 1946 which, it was proposed, would be held in June 1989. The Polish communists were guaranteed a certain percentage of seats in the *Sejm*, the lower house, but the bulk of the seats to the Senate were contested elections. Solidarity candidates won every seat they ran for, giving them control of the upper house. The April agreement also stated that the Polish president would be elected by the two houses for a six-year term, with the understanding that Jaruzelski would be named as the first President.

His first choice for Prime Minister, Czeslaw Kiszczaki, did not have enough support in Parliament to form a government, however, and he instead named Tadeuz Mazowiecki, a long-time Solidarity activist, as his candidate. When Mazowiecki was confirmed by the Polish legislature, he became the first non-Communist Prime Minister in Eastern Europe since the Czechoslovak Coup of 1948. When a political crisis threatened to emerge over the participation of the labor union in the government, Gorbachev phoned Mieczyslaw Rakowski, the First Secretary of the Polish Communist party, and urged him to cooperate with Solidarity.[4]

Both the Hungarian Round Table talks and the Polish elections were important, since they represented the beginnings of Soviet acceptance of political pluralism in Eastern Europe. Instead of sending in tanks, Gorbachev sent encouragement of and support for the reform process, even intervening to help smooth the Polish transition. They were also important because both occurred in the shadow of the Chinese government's use of force to break up pro-democracy demonstrations in Tiananmen Square on June 4, 1989. The Chinese repression was the first successful reaction by a socialist government since the introduction of Gorbachev's reform efforts.[5]

Reform in Eastern Europe acquired a new urgency after the Chinese action. Before Tiananmen Square, the East European reformers were pushing to find the limits of what was acceptable to Moscow – the so-called "Red Line" that would trigger Soviet intervention.[6] Now they sought to implement as many reforms as possible to make the process irresistible before Gorbachev either changed his mind or was replaced by someone who might emulate the Chinese clampdown.

CONTINUING WITHDRAWALS

The Soviets, for their part, accepted, or were at least resigned to, their increasing loss of hegemony over Eastern Europe. Gorbachev visited West Germany shortly after Tiananmen Square and reiterated his idea of the Common European Home and Germany's future role in it.[7] Since the Common European Home was based on peaceful relations, it seems likely that Gorbachev was trying to downplay the possibility of a Chinese-style solution for Eastern Europe.

Even more importantly, Gorbachev restated his rejection of the Brezhnev Doctrine in his speech to the Council of Europe in Strasbourg, France in July 1989. He noted that "any interference in domestic affairs and any attempts to restrict the sovereignty of states, both friends or allies or any others, are inadmissible" and he ruled out "the very possibility of the use of force or threat of forces – alliance against alliance, inside alliance, whatever."[8] The purported "Red Line" did not seem to exist, at least as far as Gorbachev was concerned. Instead, he openly approved of the reforms in Hungary and Poland.[9]

The USSR also continued with its previously announced unilateral troop reductions, including the withdrawals from the WTO states. Even before the Chinese government's crackdown, a Soviet General Staff officer stated that "the withdrawal of Soviet troops from the allied countries is proceeding strictly according to the established schedule."[10] As of June 1, 1989, the Soviet Army had withdrawn:

> more than 3,350 men and officers, 1,650 tanks, and almost 120 artillery pieces from the territory of the GDR; more than 1,000 men, 150 tanks, and more than 20 artillery pieces from the CSSR; more than 4,500 men, about 320 tanks, and 160 artillery pieces . . . from Hungary. . .[11]

These withdrawals were observed by "many military experts," as well as "representatives of a public monitoring group."[12]

Since Hungary does not border a NATO country, the Soviet troops in the country were among the least strategic European group to the USSR. The Soviets could more easily withdraw these forces and consequently the Southern command had the highest percent of the initial force reductions in Eastern Europe. A full twenty-two units of the SGF were withdrawn and disbanded, amounting to a total reduction of "more than 10,000 men, including 2,400 officers and warrant officers, more than 450 tanks, 200 guns and mortars, and 3,000 vehicles."[13] Evacuated Soviet bases were turned over to the Hungarian People's Army.

Aside from the actual numbers, the Soviets further reduced their capability of carrying out offensive action by withdrawing all ground forces units from the Hungarian–Austrian border. The only Soviet forces remaining near the border were troops assigned to the Warsaw Pact Integrated Air Defense system.[14] At the same time, the Hungarian forces were beginning their own reductions. These reductions were being carried out under the doctrinal changes called for by reasonable sufficiency.

The Soviet withdrawals were intended to be permanent, since many of the units were disbanded and the bases were turned over to the Hungarians. A commission was created "to assess the state of the military camps" and "determine their value" for any possible claims.[15] This commission also determined the future use of the buildings, which included schools or housing, which made any possible "mothballing" of facilities for any future return of the Soviet troops unlikely.[16]

Although it was claimed that the Hungarian people's response to these withdrawals was one of regret,[17] there were also calls for the total withdrawal of Soviet troops from Hungary. Shortly after these initial reductions, a member of the Alliance of Young Democrats, a group affiliated with the Alliance of Free Democrats, publicly stated that the USSR should pull its troops out. Many Hungarians viewed such a step as premature, but it was a view that would grow in popularity.[18]

Soviet acceptance of political pluralism and its continuing withdrawal from the region marked the ending of Soviet control over Eastern Europe. By refusing to intervene in either Hungary or Poland to preserve socialist rule, Gorbachev, whether intentionally or unintentionally, had "pulled the plug" on state socialism in those countries[19] and, with it, Soviet hegemony in Eastern Europe. The floodgates were now opened for the rest of the region.

EAST GERMAN CONFRONTATIONS

The events in Hungary and Poland in the spring of 1989 raised the hopes of reformers in the rest of Eastern Europe, but they also served as a warning to the other, mostly hard-line, communist leaders in the region, especially about the possible consequences of compromise for a socialist regime. These different lessons of the spring would led to increased confrontations throughout the rest of the summer and fall. At the same time, the USSR had decided to cut its losses and let Eastern Europe go, which would lead to international complications.

For East Germany, the focal point of these confrontations was the SED, or more specifically, the continued lack of legitimacy of the Honecker regime. After the East German government built the Berlin Wall in 1961, socialist rule had achieved a sort of enforced acceptance, if not legitimacy, as the last easy way out had been closed. Nevertheless, between 1961 and 1984, over 175,000 East German citizens risked imprisonment or death to flee to West Germany.[20]

The East German government employed a two-track policy to end the continuing problem of *Republikflucht* (literally, republic flight). The SED sought to improve living standards in an early version of East European consumerism and, in 1962, introduced a series of economic reforms in an attempt to make socialism work.[21] They also employed a stick to go along with the carrot, however. Severe penalties for attempting to leave illegally were established, dissident groups were placed under secret police surveillance, and shoot-to-kill orders were issued to the East German border guards.

As it turned out, these measures created a false sense of security for the largely hard-line SED leadership. Since the flow of refugees had been markedly reduced by the building of the Wall and the East German economy was, on paper at any rate, the strongest in the WTO, there seemed to be little reason to change. Yet, by 1987, that was exactly what Gorbachev was telling the Eastern European leaders. East German–Soviet relations would become increasingly strained as Gorbachev introduced more and more radical reforms in the USSR and clearly wished for the GDR to follow suit.

As *glasnost* and new thinking took hold in Moscow, the East German leaders were skeptical about the need for such policies. Honecker, visiting the USSR in June 1989, reaffirmed that the SED would not "allow well-tried things to be changed"[22] and claimed that:

> the GDR today is a modern socialist state with developed industry, agriculture, science and culture. It is marked by stability and dynamism, a high material and cultural living standard of the people, developed democracy and the rule of law, as well as social security for all.[23]

The SED secretary in charge of ideology, Kurt Hager, noted that "just because your neighbor changes his wallpaper doesn't mean that you have to."[24] More fundamentally, many of the leaders of the SED saw little or no reason to introduce Western-style reforms because it was precisely their Marxist-Leninist ideology that distinguished the country from West Germany.[25] If they introduced an East German *perestroika*, especially market mechanisms in the economy, there would be little difference between the social systems of the FRG and the GDR. Nor was there any reason for political reform since the GDR was technically already a multiparty state, albeit a controlled one. Socially, everyone's basic needs were provided for as long as one did not openly dissent.

The government's anti-reform position led many East German citizens to turn to alternative activities, including the

Lutheran Church, as a means of escape from the repression. The changes in the Hungarian government soon provided a new way out, however. In May 1989, Hungarian border guards removed the barbed wire fence between Austria and Hungary. The following summer, thousands of East German vacationers were allowed out through this new hole in the Iron Curtain.[26] In addition, GDR citizens sought refuge at West German embassies in Czechoslovakia, Hungary, Poland, and even the FRG's Permanent Representation in East Berlin. A new wave of *Republikflucht* had begun.

Despite a MfS investigation into the reasons behind this new exodus, which cited the general dissatisfaction of the people and noted the seriousness of the situation, the SED largely maintained an uncompromising position. Opposition groups, including New Forum, were formed, while established organizations were beginning to be taken over by reformers. Unlike Hungary or Poland, however, the government did not establish a dialogue with these groups, but rather relied on the use of force to put down the initial demonstrations that broke out in September.

GORBACHEV'S VISIT TO EAST BERLIN

Gorbachev was scheduled to attend East Germany's fortieth anniversary celebrations in early October 1989. Shortly before his arrival, the East Germany government allowed many of the refugees in the various West German embassies in Eastern Europe to leave on special trains. The West Germans had reportedly asked Shevardnadze to help arrange their release.[27] However, this somewhat conciliatory gesture was mitigated by the introduction of tougher visa policies.

During his visit, Gorbachev never openly called on Honecker to adopt a reform program, although his presence was clearly intended to pressure the East German leader to do so. In a meeting with the SED *Politburo* on October 7, Gorbachev all but warned Honecker on the need for change, noting that in the USSR:

we have great difficulties in the economic area, but we remain firmly committed to democracy, and we have of course learned from experience. One cannot overlook the signals of reality. Life punishes those who react too late. We've learned this from our development.[28]

Honecker reportedly ignored Gorbachev during the meeting, apparently preferring to "overlook the signals."

Tensions between Gorbachev and Honecker increased during the visit. Gorbachev supposedly told Honecker that he was aware of Honecker's attempt to establish a de-facto alliance among the remaining hard-line communist states, which would have included the GDR, Czechoslovakia, Romania, and even the People's Republic of China, along with hard-line elements in the USSR, and that this course of action was unacceptable.[29] He also called on the East German populace to decide the issue of reform.[30]

As had happened earlier that year in Beijing, and as he most likely figured would happen if he went to the GDR, Gorbachev's arrival was seized by pro-reform groups as an opportunity to press for greater freedoms. Despite the MfS's extensive security precautions, the demonstrations continued throughout the country, as an East German version of "Gorbymania" swept the opposition groups, who called on Gorbachev to intervene against the Honecker regime.[31] Thousands of East German protesters were arrested.

Gorbachev also took a more active role in pressuring the East German communists. As he was leaving the GDR, he reportedly told pro-reform members of the SED *Politburo*, "*deistvuite*" ("take action").[32] The KGB, in conjunction with the MfS, was already helping to undermine the authority of the East German hard-liners by supporting the activities of more independent, reform-minded GDR *bezirke* (East German districts) officials.[33] If Honecker and other similar-minded East Germans would not change, then Gorbachev would find "supporters of *perestroika*"[34] elsewhere.

Most importantly, he played his trump card, the Soviet forces in the country, which had been redesignated as *Zapadnaya Gruppa Voisk* (the Western Group of Forces).

Gorbachev ordered the Soviet troops to stay in their barracks regardless of the domestic situation in the GDR.[35] Since the authority of the SED ultimately rested on the nineteen divisions of the WGF, Gorbachev's order meant that Honecker had lost his most powerful sanction. It also meant that the East German communists were on their own. There would not be a repeat of 1953.

THE CHINA SYNDROME

On October 9, after Gorbachev had left for Moscow, Honecker met with the Chinese Vice Premier, Yao Yilin. East German–Chinese relations had markedly improved in the late 1980s, especially after the GDR supported the Chinese government after its crackdown against the demonstrators in Tiananmen Square.[36] Faced with continuing demonstrations against his own regime, Honecker was most likely looking for support of a similar action on his part.

Honecker warned the pro-democracy protesters not "to destablize socialist construction or slander its achievements,"[37] while preparing for a *"Chinesische Losung"* (Chinese solution). Riot police, secret police, *Kampfgruppen* militia, and NVA units were ordered into the East German city of Leipzig, where demonstrations had continued after Gorbachev's departure. Medical facilities were readied to deal with the wounded. A SED *Politburo* order authorizing the use of force to suppress that evening's demonstration was purportedly issued the same day.

The attack never came, however. The "Monday demonstration" of over 70,000 people came and went. According to some accounts, local officials, in cooperation with leaders of the Leipzig pro-democracy movement, contravened the order.[38] Since the planned assault included the use of East German airborne troops, a local countermand would seem unlikely since the paratroopers would have been controlled from the Ministry of Defense Headquarters in East Berlin. It has also been claimed that Egon Krenz, the member of the

SED *Politburo* in charge of national security, intervened and countermanded the attack order.[39]

The WGF may have also played a role in the events at Leipzig. Willy Brandt, the former West German chancellor, claimed that the WGF command interceded to prevent the planned attack.[40] Soviet officers urged their NVA counterparts not to use force against civilians, while, at the same time, making it clear that the WGF would remain in their barracks if the NVA went along with Honecker's "Tiananmen Square solution."[41] It was also reported that tank units of the WGF actually blocked NVA bases in the Leipzig area to prevent the East German forces from assisting in any crackdown.[42] Given that Soviet officers worked closely with the NVA,[43] the WGF was at least in a position to know what was going on and to relay this information back to Moscow.

The combination of the continuing demonstrations, lower level bureaucratic resistance, and the lack of Soviet support led to an emergency meeting of the SED *Politburo* the following day. The East German leaders were now divided as several members realized that East Germany had to change and the SED would have to accept reforms.[44] Hager, the party ideologue, quickly flew to Moscow for consultations with the Soviets. After his return, he announced the convening of a special party congress, which would feature "a large open discussion" of the GDR's problems.[45]

The demonstrations, meanwhile, continued throughout East Germany. Some local officials entered into direct talks with opposition groups, including the still-illegal New Forum.[46] The SED was beginning to lose control of the situation. In response, Krenz and Gunther Schabowski arranged Honecker's resignation as first secretary, with Krenz taking over as the party leader. Although the Soviet ambassador to the GDR was kept informed of the impending change, the Soviets did not intervene as they had in Ulbricht's ouster in 1970. Shevardnadze responded to Honecker's resignation by reaffirming the Soviets' nonintervention policy.[47]

The SED, unlike the Chinese communists, effectively capitulated when it was faced with a confrontation with opposition forces.[48] The hard-liners did not or could not carry through with a decisive use of force and Honecker, one of the major proponents of a Chinese-type action, was forcibly retired. The more moderate members of the East German *Politburo* opted against force. For his part, Gorbachev had not only refuted the Brezhnev Doctrine – he had effectively turned it on its head. Instead of intervening militarily to preserve an orthodox socialist regime, the USSR now openly supported the reformers and quite possibly intervened on their side in the ensuing struggle.

THE FALL OF THE WALL

Honecker's resignation did not stop the demonstrations, which actually increased in size throughout the fall. For all intents and purposes, the ouster was a "palace coup" within the SED to try to make it more palatable to the growing opposition forces. Krenz, who had publicly supported the Chinese government's action in Tiananmen Square in June, now portrayed himself as a reform communist who would introduce a "policy of renewal" in the GDR.[49]

This socialist renewal involved the introduction of a more democratic government, although the SED would retain its monopoly of power, and the continued sovereignty of the GDR. Reunification was not an issue for the new leadership. Rather, the major interest in unifying the two Germanies was in the FRG's leadership.[50] On the other hand, SED officials now met regularly with members of the opposition groups, including a meeting between Schabowski and New Forum representatives in late October.[51]

Krenz sought support for his reforms both domestically and internationally. He asked Hans Modrow, the SED party head in the city of Dresden and a major advocate of reform, to play a greater role in the party's leadership.[52] Krenz also visited Moscow in early November to meet with Gorbachev and stopped in Warsaw on the way back. The Soviets were openly pleased with the turn of events in East Germany, but reaffirmed that East German matters "are decided not in Moscow, but in Berlin."[53] Upon his return, Krenz again appealed for time to institute his policies. Time, however, was something he did not have.

The demonstrations continued on an increasingly larger scale. The now traditional Monday night demonstrations in Leipzig were reaching upwards of 300,000 people. In early November, an estimated 500,000 demonstrators attended a rally in East Berlin. Instead of giving the SED a respite to carry out their renewal, the opposition forces were pushing for even greater reforms, including the freedom of travel.[54] Many East German citizens were leaving in spite of the continuing restrictions.

In response, the government began to ease travel restrictions. Initially, they introduced an amnesty for violations of the travel laws, which was quickly followed by the lifting of restrictions of travel from Czechoslovakia to the FRG.[55] In a last, and largely futile, gesture, the GDR Ministry of the Interior then announced that East Germans would be allowed up to thirty days abroad each year. None of these moves stopped the new exodus. The inability of the government to deal with the demonstrations or the emigration did, however, play a key role in the resignation of the entire SED *Politburo* on November 8.

Krenz, Schabowski, and other former members, made up most of the reconstituted *Politburo*, however, with Krenz retaining the party leadership. More important, though, Modrow was appointed to the new body and nominated as the new prime minister. The first thing the new leadership did, inadvertently as it turned out, was to open the inner-German border. On November 9, Schabowski announced a new travel decree, which included a gradual opening of the borders, but which was quickly interpreted as allowing free travel.[56] The misunderstanding turned the previous demonstrations into celebrations as Berliners from both sides converged on the Berlin Wall.

The East German government apparently attempted to reverse the situation by ordering the NVA's 1st Motorized-Rifle Division to re-close the Berlin Wall on November 11. The order, which would have required authorization by Krenz, was never carried out as the division's command staff questioned both the feasibility of actually getting their troops to carry out the order and their own convictions in doing so. The NVA General Staff also began to question the order.[57] The East German military was now divided over the question of reform.

The decision to go along with the opening of the borders was largely a domestic one, albeit one forced on the SED by the demonstrations. The Soviets did not directly involve themselves, although, as happened in both Hungary and Poland before a far-reaching reform, Gorbachev was consulted prior to the event.[58] The opening of the Wall did not stop either the refugees or the demands for change, however. Gorbachev reportedly sent Valentin Falin, the head of the International Department of the CPSU Secretariat, to East Berlin to help arrange a transfer of power from Krenz to Modrow.[59] Modrow was elected chairman of the Council of Ministers, or the prime minister, in a coalition government on November 17.[60]

Like Krenz, Modrow was committed to reforming socialism in the GDR. East Germany was to have "a government of the people and of labor. It will be a government of peace and socialism."[61] He was more willing to reach out to the opposition forces, especially since the constitutional provisions for the SED's monopoly of power had been removed, and to promote democracy. This was almost exactly what at least one of the opposition groups had stated earlier.[62]

Modrow was also committed to the continued existence of the GDR as a sovereign state, although he was "prepared to develop its cooperation with the FRG and to place it on a new, higher level."[63] At the same time, East Germany would maintain its ties to the WTO states, especially those with the USSR.[64] In terms of defense issues, East Germany would continue to seek "peace, detente and disarmament in Europe."[65] The NVA was to be reformed, including the democratization of the military.

Modrow's reforms, however, had very little chance of success. The mass emigrations continued and the economy was now near a state of collapse, in part due to the exodus of skilled labor. The SED held its extraordinary party congress in December 1989 in an attempt to deal with the critical

situation. The former leadership was held responsible for it
failure to use "its opportunities to make amendments to the
party course."[66] The SED formally divested itself o
"command and bureaucratic methods" at the congress
renaming itself the Socialist Unity Party-the Party o
Democratic Socialism (SED-PDS).[67] The new party chairman
Gregor Gysi, reiterated the party's commitment to socialis
renewal.

THE RISE OF THE OPPOSITION

Despite the rapid changes in the government and the party
and Modrow's efforts to move the center of power to the
government, the SED-PDS was still losing what little
authority it had. The West Germans did not consider then
as having "any chances" of being successful.[68] The Wes
German Social Democrats, who had extensive contacts with
the East German party, even broke off relations with the
SED-PDS, shifting their support to the newly-formed Socia
Democratic Party of the GDR.[69]

The opposition forces continued their protests in major Eas
German cities, but these demonstrations, including those led
by New Forum, were now sanctioned by the government.[70]
The opposition called for several reforms, which included free
elections, the equality of all political parties, control over the
MfS, equality for women, freedom of the press, and ecologica
concerns.[71] East Germany society was becoming more and
more "politicized."[72]

At the head of this politicization was the New Forum
movement which, like the Hungarian Democratic Forum, was
largely an umbrella organization for many different opposition groups. It was not the only one, as other groups such as
Alliance-90, Democratic Awakening, and New Democracy
had also formed, while several of the former "brotherly"
organizations such as the trade unions or SED-allied parties
elected new, independent leaders. In the East German
Christian Democratic Union (CDU), for example, Lothar de

Maiziere was named the new head of the party, replacing the SED-approved candidate.

These opposition forces generally wanted a faster rate of reform, although not necessarily the complete abandonment of socialism. Like the government, these groups, and the population as a whole, were not generally interested in an early reunification with the FRG. Shortly after Modrow took over, seventy percent of East Germans supported continued statehood for the GDR, although the same poll noted that eighty percent thought that the economy was "very bad."[73]

Reunification, however, would not go away as an issue, largely due to the state of the economy. Modrow would eventually propose a "treaty community" between the two Germanies, "which would include important confederative elements such as a union in economy, currency, and transport, and rapprochement in legal sphere."[74] Just as the hard-liners in the SED had feared, however, even discussions of joining with a market economy diminished the GDR's authority. The opposition forces were now in the ascendancy.

Starting in December 1989, an East German "roundtable" was held between the "parties and organizations involved in government, plus new GDR movements and groupings."[75] These talks would eventually culminate in the drafting of a new East German constitution. The draft text stressed the rights of citizens, to an even greater extent that the West German Basic Law.[76] Although it was quickly eclipsed by the East German elections and subsequent expansion of the unification process, the roundtable's text did seek to establish a law-based state.

The SED-PDS attempted to position themselves as "just one of the political forces in the country"[77] before the elections in March. They dropped the letters SED from their name in February 1990 in an attempt to dissociate the party from its past. The attempts to reform the party may not have been entirely successful, however. A purported PDS protocol was published in a West German magazine, which noted that the PDS had falsified records to protect the identities of MfS members and was prepared to destroy incriminating files in the event of reunification.[78]

The destruction of files in the central registration office for judicial crimes of the GDR in the town of Salzgitter supposedly would have been a joint action of the GDR and the USSR.[79] Unidentified East German forces were to be assisted by "Soviet specialists," presumably KGB or Soviet military intelligence operatives.[80] Units of the WGF may have also been involved in the dissolution of the MfS.[81] Regardless of the accuracy of these reports, the USSR was clearly supporting the East German government.

DEFENDING THE GAINS OF "GOOD SOCIALISM"

The Soviets viewed the East German revolution much as they looked upon the reform process in the USSR. The events of the fall were the result of "a crisis of the administrative command system in its GDR incarnation."[82] The East German developments, moreover, were largely the result of *perestroika*. The changes "in the GDR would be unthinkable without Soviet *perestroika*, without the enormous reforms in the Soviet Union. In any case, not in the way, in this beneficial way, it has taken place."[83]

Strategically, therefore, there was every reason for the Soviets to "still consider the GDR as our main ally, as a fraternal socialist country."[84] It was also economically important to the USSR, which had "invested a lot into the coming into being and consolidation of this country."[85] In addition to maintaining its bilateral ties to the USSR, the East German government reaffirmed its commitment to the Warsaw Pact in a meeting of the WTO defense ministers in late November, despite the political changes.[86]

At these meetings, Theodor Hoffman, the East German defense minister, also announced a military reform program for the NVA. As a means of implementing reasonable sufficiency, the NVA would be reduced in size, "but more modern and well-led" to "guarantee a reliable defense in the national framework and within the alliance."[87] The NVA was to become more accountable to elected bodies, while living

:onditions for conscripts in the NVA were to be improved.
'Democratic consultations" were being carried out in the
military instead of political indoctrination.[88]

The WGF continued to serve as a bulwark for the new
government. Even with Gorbachev's unilateral force reduc-
ions, the presence of 360,000 Soviet troops in East Germany
guaranteed the GDR's sovereignty. In a meeting between
Modrow and Army General Boris Sntekov, the commander-
n-chief of the WGF, Modrow emphasized the role of the
WGF in the "strengthening of the country's stability."[89] The
:wo militaries continued to cooperate, which included holding
oint exercises in the GDR.[90] WGF soldiers even assisted in
'helping the Republic's national economy," by providing free
abor in East German communities.[91]

Not every one was interested in aiding the new government's stability, however. The GDR department for the
safeguarding of constitutional rights, an East German copy of
e West German Office for the Protection of the Constitu-
:ion, reported that American and West German intelligence
nad increased their activities in the GDR after the opening of
the border.[92] The western services were reportedly taking
advantage of the decline in East German counterintelligence
:apabilities to infiltrate GDR organizations and "to discredit
leading GDR statesmen."[93]

The goal of these purported covert operations was to
prevent East Germany from moving ahead with its reforms, so
as to prepare for a more rapid reunification with the FRG,
and to prevent "the growth of the influence of the political
forces advocating the renewal of socialism."[94] The Soviets
"expressed support for the people and the government of the
GDR, which emphatically reject interference in their internal
affairs."[95]

RENEWAL AND REVOLUTION

The events in Hungary, Poland, and East Germany served as a
:atalyst for change in the rest of the WTO states. As will be
discussed in Chapter 5, Czechoslovakia, Bulgaria, and even

Romania, all changed their leaders, if not the actual government, and introduced some sort of reform package. The Soviets initially tended to think of this process as a renewal of socialism, along the lines of the Soviet reform effort.[96]

Gorbachev had to have been reasonably pleased with the turn of events in Eastern Europe by the end of year. Not only had the other WTO states begun to change, with the attendant possibility of actually becoming viable allies, but several of the major embarrassments of the region, notably the Berlin Wall and the Romanian leader, Nicolae Ceausescu, were gone. Eastern Europe was moving along "the same main direction" as the USSR, with minimal Soviet involvement.[97] New thinking in Eastern Europe was an apparent success.

Of course, Gorbachev would soon be faced with the same problem he had in Soviet politics, namely the inability to control the forces he had set in motion. Once the peoples of Eastern Europe had their independence from a one-party system, many of them wanted nothing to do with socialism. The process of a renewal frequently became a revolution as western ideas were introduced into the political systems of several of the WTO states. East Germany would take this revolution one step further and actually vote itself out of existence.

5 The WGF and Moscow's Relations with Germany

Set your entreatments at a higher rate/Than a command to parle
> – William Shakespeare, *Hamlet*, Act I, scene iii

The changes in Eastern Europe were widely held to mark the end of the Cold War. The USSR accepted limited political pluralism in the other countries of the WTO and cooperated more with the United States and Western Europe. These acts were largely the result of the Soviet reforms and were, for the most part, intended consequences of new thinking. In the case of Eastern Europe, however, many of the new governments quickly began to move away from reform socialism and looked to develop closer ties with the West.

From a theoretical perspective, the loosening ties within the WTO was a rough equivalent to the deconcentration phase of a long cycle, which is characterized by shifting alliances away from the dominant power. As the non-Soviet states began to move further away from the Soviet model, the alliance began to weaken. In his attempt to strengthen the pact, Gorbachev had set in motion events that reduced the Soviets' military position in the region. None of the countries represented this shift of allegiance away from the USSR better than East Germany, which would, in rapid fashion, become part of the Federal Republic.

This chapter will look at this process, in particular the German reunification, Soviet relations with the various Germanies, and relations between the WGF and Germany. Given the magnitude of these changes, none of them has been easy. In addition to domestic problems relating to the entire unification, Germany also had cause for concern over the WGF.

EASTERN EUROPE DOMINOES

The events in East Germany marked the turning point in Soviet policy towards Eastern Europe. If the Soviets could accept and even promote democratization in their most important ally, then there was little reason for supporting the remaining orthodox socialist regimes in Bulgaria, Czechoslovakia and Romania. As had happened to the Honecker regime, these socialist governments were now basically on their own as the Soviets opted for actual reform.

The Berlin Wall had barely been opened before the changes in Eastern Europe continued. Peaceful demonstrations, which had worked so well in East Germany, were becoming commonplace occurrences in Czechoslovakia. Like the New Forum movement in the GDR, Civic Forum, the Czechoslovak opposition umbrella organization, largely organized and led these protests. The Czechoslovak communists under Jakes, like Honecker, refused to negotiate with the opposition forces and initially relied on the use of force in an attempt to put down the demonstrations.

The use of force, in contrast to the more peaceful transitions in Hungary, Poland, and eventually in the GDR, further diminished international support for the Czechoslovak government. Even Hungary, a WTO ally, criticized the Czechoslovak government's handling of the protests. Gorbachev, who continued to rule out any military interventions to save the remaining regimes, sought to pressure Jakes by warning him that the USSR was in the process of reconsidering the events of 1968 and would likely condemn the WTO "interference" with the Prague Spring.

Without any sort of support, either domestically or internationally, the Czechoslovak government capitulated to the opposition, effectively handing power over to Civic Forum. Vaclav Havel, a Czech playwright who had been

mprisoned for dissident activities, was named acting pre-
ident. The Czechoslovak reformers instituted a series of
eforms intended to move the country away from socialism.
Meanwhile, demonstrations in Bulgaria, largely by ethnic
Turks who were protesting the Bulgarian government's forced
assimilation program, and elite dissatisfaction with the party
first secretary, Todor Zhivkov, led to Zhivkov's ouster. This
"palace coup," was led by Zhivkov's foreign minister, Petur
Mladenov.[1]

Unlike in Czechoslovakia, where he played a more indirect
ole, Gorbachev may have been directly involved in Zhivkov's
removal.[2] At any rate, he clearly supported Mladenov. The
events in Bulgaria were different from what had occurred so
far in the other WTO states, since it was much more of a
change within the party than the inclusion of opposition
forces. Nevertheless, Mladenov did move to implement
reforms for "the long-overdue profound democratic transfor-
mations" of Bulgarian politics and society.[3]

By the middle of December 1989, Romania was the last
hard-line socialist state in the WTO. Ceausescu, the party
leader, relied on Stalinist methods, including a personality cult
and the use of terror enforced by his secret police, the
Securitate, to stay in power. Like Zhivkov in Bulgaria,
Ceausescu also forced minorities, including ethnic Hungarians, to assimilate themselves into the dominant Romanian
culture. When protests in the largely ethnic-Hungarian town
of Timosaora broke out over the arrest of a Hungarian
Reformed Church priest, the Romanian government sent in
the army and the secret police to suppress them.

Word of the demonstrations and the government's use of
force got out, however, as the events had been videotaped.
The protests spread to other Romanian towns, including the
capital city of Bucharest. When the Romanian army refused
to intervene against the demonstrators, Ceausescu had the
defense minister executed. The army then joined with the
demonstrators in seeking Ceasescu's ouster. The defection of
the military led to a short-lived civil war as the *Securitate*
fought to keep Ceausescu in power against the people and the
army.

Ceausescu and his wife were captured by army troops on Christmas Day, tried in a military court, convicted and summarily executed. The *Securitate* fought on briefly, but eventually surrendered. The National Salvation Front, a coalition movement which was largely controlled by Romanian communists, took over with Ion Iliescu as president. As in Bulgaria, the principal change was the removal of a long term party leader who resisted reform. In both cases, the upheaval was directed against the orthodox socialist system within the country and not necessarily against the USSR.

Once again, the Soviets had to be relatively relieved by these further changes in Eastern Europe. The last of the hard-line regimes in the WTO were gone and, despite the changes, the security commitment "assumed under the Warsaw Pact . . . remains in force. Nobody has backed down."[4] The Soviets alliance had withstood the opening up of the Eastern European party-state systems. Shevardnadze recognized that this situation may not last, however, and that the "time may come when it is necessary to look again at things."[5]

In some cases, especially in Polish–Soviet relations, the change to a non-socialist government almost seemed to improve relations, at least at first. Well after Solidarity's electoral victory, the Soviets felt "that relations between the Soviet Union and Poland are generally developing in a satisfactory fashion,"[6] which even included the continued presence of the Soviet Northern Group of Forces (NGF) in Polish territory. After the East German revolution, the Poles would begin to worry about their western borders and to look on the Soviet troops as their "best guarantee."[7]

Not every Polish citizen agreed with the government's analysis, however. Polish youths demonstrated in front of NGF bases yelling " 'Soviets go home' and 'tanks to the Volga River.' "[8] In both Hungary and Czechoslovakia, the new governments began pressing the Soviets to completely withdraw their forces. In both cases, the Soviets eventually agreed signing agreements with each government. The first Soviet units, aircraft based at Debrecen, left Hungary on March 20, 1990.[9] In Czechoslovakia, the agreement was negotiated while protests over the presence of the Soviet troops broke out in

Prague.[10] The time for looking again at things was apparently coming.

QUESTIONS OF UNIFICATION

The reunification of Germany never really disappeared as an issue, even after the start of the Cold War. It was written into the Basic Law of the FRG and many German citizens wished for it. Reunification was downgraded as an issue during the years of SPD rule, but when the Christian Democratic Union regained control of the government in 1982, the old hopes re-emerged. Even before the dramatic changes in the East German government, Helmut Kohl, the West German chancellor, apparently decided, in light of the reforms in Hungary, Poland, and the USSR, "that the time for resolute action" had arrived.[11]

The beginnings of another mass exodus of East Germans only reinforced the reunification question. West German officials were concerned that if people continued to leave the GDR, reunification would take place in the FRG. Honecker's removal and the subsequent changes in the East German government actually increased the flow of refugees.[12] These events only led to further talks on reunification, both within West Germany and in Europe.

Shortly after Modrow was named prime minister, the *Bundestag*, the lower house of the West German parliament, debated the possibility of reunification. Despite the idealistic goal, the realities of merging two different social systems also began to set in. In the first place, reunification would be expensive for West Germany. Not only would the integration of the East German economic infrastructure into the FRG cost money to bring the eastern companies up to West German standards, but the merging of the two currencies could represent a drain on the *deutschemark*.

Socially, the East Germans might have a difficult time being integrated into a capitalistic society. On the other hand, West Germans would suddenly be faced with a cheaper source of labor in the country, also possibly increasing tensions.[13] These potentially negative consequences led many West Germans to adopt a go-slow approach to the problem and let relations between the FRG and the GDR normalize. They were not the only ones, as other European states, many of which had suffered from German aggression in World War II, also voiced caution.

In spite of the economic and military integration of the Federal Republic with much of the rest of Western Europe, and especially with the French, its European partners were nervous. Two of the more concerned countries were, para- doxically, two of West Germany's major allies, Britain and France. The British government openly "linked the prospect of German unification with notions of a 'Fourth Reich.' "[14] The French government was not only worried about Germany's aggressive past, but also about the economic potential of an united Germany with a population of 80 million.[15]

Neither Britain or France, however, had annexed German territory after World War II. Poland and the USSR had divided East Prussia, while Poland took the regions of Pomerania and Silesia as compensation for the westward adjustment of the Polish–Soviet border. Millions of Germans were forced from their homes following the annexations. Consequently, both Poland and the USSR were concerned about possible German attempts to recover these "pre-1937" lands. Ambiguous West German statements about what would constitute an united Germany did not allay these fears.[16]

As noted, the Solidarity-dominated Polish government viewed the continued presence of Soviet troops in Germany as a guarantee of their post-war borders. The Soviets had the additional worry of the entire post-war European order they had helped maintain. The Soviets' primary concern was keeping the peace. The key to the long peace in Europe after World War II, as they saw it, was the military balance that existed between the two alliances. German reunification, especially a process where East Germany would simply join West Germany, represented a threat to that balance.[17]

A second, and related, problem was interference in East German affairs. As already noted, the Soviets were concerned that Western intelligence agencies were attempting to destabilize the GDR, even after the introduction of the reforms. In their view, unification, if it were to occur, should be an act between two sovereign states.[18] In both cases, the Soviets considered that any possible reunification should be part of a greater pan-European process, which would guarantee European stability.

The people who wanted a quick reunification were Kohl, American officials, and ultimately the East Germans. Kohl saw a reasonably quick unification as the only real solution to the continuing East German refugee problem. West Germany did attempt to help stabilize the East German economy through increased cooperation, but the exodus continued. The American president, George Bush, and secretary of state, James Baker, openly supported Kohl's efforts and privately pressured both Britain and France to accept unification.[19]

The people who really decided the issue, however, were the East Germans themselves. As the East German economy verged on collapse, many of them physically left, or at least wanted to. At one point, almost one-third of the country had applied for an exit visa. They were, to use Lenin's words, voting with their feet. The combination of the economic and refugee problems continued to plague the effectiveness of Modrow's government. Free elections were scheduled for March 18, 1990 as a means of resolving the impasse.

Some of the opposition groups, such as Alliance-90, which was affiliated with the Green movement, would re-establish themselves as political parties, but the major parties were the previously junior members of the SED-dominated government. The two principal parties were the East German CDU and SPD, both of which received money and assistance from their West German counterparts. The CDU, under de Maiziere, won a near-majority in their own right and promptly announced the formation of a "Grand Coalition" with the SPD and most of the other parties, with de Maiziere as prime minister. The PDS, which won only eleven percent of the vote, was excluded from the coalition.

With the same ruling party in power in both Germanies, it was a question of when reunification would occur, rather than if it would. The FRG and the GDR took the initial step towards unification when they merged their economies on June 1, 1990. It was this economic, monetary, and social union that finally stopped the East German exodus.[20] The two governments began negotiations on a unification treaty. The major stumbling blocks were now international concerns, especially the continued occupation status of Berlin, membership in military alliances, and the presence of the WGF.

THE 2 + 4 CONFERENCE

The conclusion of the European part of World War II was somewhat unusual for a major war in that there was no formal peace treaty. The four wartime allies still technically occupied the city of Berlin. The Americans, British, and the French maintained forces in the city and, although the Soviets did not base troops in the western part, they did keep an honor guard at the Soviet war memorial in the British sector and they still had transit rights. If Germany was to be reunited, the four powers would have to surrender these rights.

The actual process of redefining the occupation status of Berlin began after the formation of the Modrow government. The former wartime allies meet to discuss what was known as "the Berlin initiative" of the western powers, which concerned the occupation status. The Soviet ambassador to the GDR, Vyacheslav Kochemasov, attended, as did high level representatives of the other three occupation states.[21] These initial talks were largely the result of the changes in the GDR, which had dropped its insistence of an independent political status for West Berlin within the FRG.[22]

As unification became more likely, the four powers, along with the two German states, declared their intentions to convene talks known as the 2 + 4 Conference to discuss "all international aspects of Germany's reunification."[23] The Polish government requested representation at the meetings, and while they were initially turned down, Gorbachev made it clear that the USSR would look out for Polish interests.[24] The Soviets also noted that they treated "with full seriousness the rights and responsibility of the four powers in German affairs."[25]

The first round of the talks, which took place in Bonn, quickly bogged down on the future allegiance of a reunified Germany. Kohl, with American support, wanted to keep Germany in NATO while the Soviets wanted either German neutrality or, at least, membership of both NATO and the WTO. Gennady Shikin, Kochemasov's successor in East Berlin, explicitly ruled out "full German membership in NATO,"[26] a position echoed by East German officials.[27] Marshal Sergey Akhromeyev, Gorbachev's defense advisor, stated "that a reunified Germany cannot belong to any military bloc."[28]

The Soviets also still preferred that the question of German unity be part of a larger pan-European peace system, since any reunification had to be "compatible with the security interests of all nations in Europe, including the security interests of the Germans themselves."[29] One component of this new European security arrangement would be the withdrawal of foreign troops, including Soviet forces, from all countries. As far as the WGF was concerned, the USSR did not "need a military presence either in a Germany of two states or in a united Germany."[30]

Both Kohl and Bush saw little need for such a solution. The WTO would soon be disbanded and was only being kept around to "clear up this mess," as de Maiziere reported to Bush when the two met in June 1990.[31] Due to the ongoing withdrawals, the USSR's strategic position in Europe was at its weakest point since World War II. Nevertheless, the Soviets viewed an unified Germany in NATO to be such a threat to the stability of the European balance that they apparently considered launching a pre-emptive military strike.[32]

At least twice, in the fall of 1989 and the winter of 1990, high level discussions about such an option were supposed to have taken place among the Soviet leadership. The USSR "would consider using military force to prevent reunification on unacceptable terms."[33] Such an intervention, if one were actually considered, would have relied heavily on the WGF, even though it was now in a relatively isolated position and far less capable of conducting a deep operation against NATO.

Fortunately, the Soviets chose to negotiate rather than fight. Gorbachev presented a revised plan, which was also supported by de Maiziere, for German membership in NATO in which the territory of the GDR was "to be given special status for a transitional period," until a pan-European solution was set up.[34] During this period, no NATO troops would be deployed on the territory of the former GDR, while the WGF would remain. Furthermore, this special status would be contracted to by NATO and the WTO.[35] As part of the plan, both alliances would become political organizations and eventually be eliminated.

The 2 + 4 talks adjourned without a solution to the problem of NATO membership. The diplomatic effort now shifted to personal negotiations between Kohl and Gorbachev, which were scheduled for July. The German chancellor and the Soviet president would have to find a compromise between the growing realities of German unification and the ever-present possibility of a Soviet veto.

POWER POLITICS

The major problem the Soviets had with German membership in NATO was the orientation of the alliance. Despite the changes in Eastern Europe and the USSR, the Soviets felt it was still largely directed against them. While this situation was workable due to the current understandings, things can change, as the events of 1989 had so amply demonstrated. The leaders of the NATO countries held a summit meeting in London in June 1990 to address the future of the organization and came out in favor of the future politicization of the organization.

The London Summit cleared the way for the success of Gorbachev–Kohl talks. Kohl went to Moscow "at a remarkable time."[36] Both countries were going through dramatic changes. Moreover, the changes were linked since it was Gorbachev's reforms that had led to the possibility of German reunification.[37] Just as important, both sides had something the other wanted. The Soviets wanted economic assistance from the West, and especially from West Germany, while the Germans wanted Soviet acquiescence for unification. About the only issues left were security questions.

After initial discussions in Moscow, Gorbachev took Kohl to his home town region of Stavropol. In what Gorbachev would term "*Realpolitik*" (power politics), the two leaders reached an agreement over the major international concerns. The USSR dropped its objection to continued German membership in NATO, while the German government accepted the deployment of the WGF in the territory of the GDR up to the end of 1994. A German–Soviet treaty would be negotiated although it would not go into effect until after German unification.

Specifically, Kohl and Gorbachev agreed that, although the FRG would stay in NATO, no German units assigned to NATO would be stationed in what had been East Germany until the Soviet withdrawal was completed.[38] The only forces that could be stationed there during the transitional period would be "German eastern territorial forces," which would be established out of the former NVA, and the Western allies' units in West Berlin.[39] The territorial units, totaling 50,000 to 70,000 soldiers, would be part of the German *Bundeswehr* but would not be assigned to the NATO command structure.[40] Even after the Soviet withdrawal, non-German NATO units could not be based in eastern Germany.

The unified German military would be reduced to 370,000 men, down from approximately 480,000 in the West German military and 160,000 in the NVA, in the same time period. The East German defense treaties would have to be canceled or updated by the signatories.[41] In addition, Germany would reaffirm its international treaty commitments not to possess biological, chemical or nuclear weapons, nor would any NATO nuclear weapons be allowed east of the Elbe river, even after the Soviets had left.[42]

The WGF would have to withdraw by the end of 1994, but the West German government would pay for its maintenance on German territory, transportation costs to the Soviet border, re-education for the servicemen, and assistance in building housing for the relocated troops and their dependents in the USSR during that time.[43] In addition, the German government would guarantee three billion dollars in bank credits to the USSR.[44] The total "unification price" for the West Germans would be approximately 10 billion dollars by the time the Soviet troops were out.

It was a small price to pay since the Gorbachev–Kohl agreement, referred to as "Stavrapallo" by an East German official,[45] allowed the two Germanies to reunite. In actuality, the West Germans "would have agreed to anything" to get the Soviets' acceptance.[46] The final international problem was dealt with the day after Gorbachev's and Kohl's announcement, when West Germany accepted a compromise over the borders of an unified Germany and stated that it would sign a treaty with Poland recognizing the Oder–Neisse line as Germany's eastern border shortly after unification.[47]

Germany and the other Western powers also agreed to expand the role of the Conference on Security and Cooperation in Europe (CSCE) following the conclusion of the 2 + 4 Conference. The CSCE, which was established in 1975 as part of the Helsinki Accords, was intended to become the pan-European security system to maintain the balance. The scheduled meeting of the CSCE in November 1990 would formally note the agreements of the conference, as well as start creating institutional structures to deal with its increased responsibilities.

Although Gorbachev did not get everything he wanted out of the talks at Stavropol, he got much of what he could expect. NATO had earlier agreed in principle to move in the direction he wanted, Germany would reunify on terms that were acceptable, if not exactly optimal, to the USSR, the unification would take place within an European framework, he would get much-needed financial assistance, and, above all else, Soviet security was not compromised. Soviet troops would not only remain in Germany and Poland for the time being, but the American forces would not advance.

Kohl presumably could have waited for the Soviet position in Eastern Europe to collapse, when he might have achieved unification much more cheaply. By July, it was apparent that both were going to happen eventually. But that could have possibly represented a higher price than the ten billion dollars. Hard-line communists were attempting to reassert the power of the center in the USSR and Gorbachev's authority was weakening. Like the East Europeans, Kohl also wanted to make as many reforms as possible while Gorbachev was still in power.

ASSENT AND ACCESSION

Technically, all that remained in the way of German unification were legalities. The 2 + 4 Conference would have to draft a treaty, while the two Germanies would also have to agree on the terms of the reunification. In addition, the Soviet and West German governments needed to negotiate a treaty formalizing the Gorbachev-Kohl agreement. The diplomats and negotiators had taken over from the heads of states.

With the international questions largely answered, the major focus turned to the method and nature of the unification process. As noted, representatives of the FRG and the GDR met to create a 900-page treaty that covered almost all of the aspects of the reunification. The most important feature was that East Germany would accede to article 23 of the West German Basic Law on midnight, October 3, 1990, with the territory of the GDR becoming part of the FRG. Article 23 of the Basic Law would then be revised so as to preclude the rest of pre-1937 territory.

The unification treaty was signed in East Berlin by de Maiziere and Kohl on August 31, 1990. Wolfgang Schauble, the FRG interior minister who led the negotiations for West Germany, noted that reunification could now "proceed in an orderly fashion."[48] Even before the actual signing, the West Germans announced that a *Bundeswehr* unit would be transferred to Berlin after unification,[49] while the federal cabinet approved the continued presence of foreign troops, including those of the WGF, in Berlin,[50] although the foreign troops would lose their special rights, including extraterritoriality.

Even before, the 2 + 4 Conference had reconvened in East Berlin to finalized the details of the Treaty on the Final Settlement on Germany, otherwise known as the 2 + 4 Treaty. The draft document called for complete German sovereignty after the reunification and established a December 31, 1994 deadline for the Soviet withdrawal. In addition, a supplemental letter to be signed by the two Germanies was added, stating that "a united Germany will not restore Nazi ideologies."[51] The supplement also covered the maintenance of Soviet war memorials in the GDR.

The talks between the diplomatic and military experts then adjourned and the conference moved to Moscow for a meeting of the foreign ministers of the six countries and the formal signing ceremony. The Soviets and the East German had already begun to act as if the treaty was in place, as the Soviet 8th Tank Division started its withdrawal from its base at Neuruppin,[52] while East Germany began to destroy ammunition[53] and ended foreign military training for NVA personnel.[54] It was also rumored that the Soviets dismantled and moved high technology East German firms, including the Zeiss camera works, to the USSR. These claims, however, proved to be unfounded.[55]

The major last hurdle to unification concerned the WGF, or more specifically the amount of money the Federal Republic would pay for their continued stationing in and withdrawal from the soon-to-be-former GDR. The West German foreign minister, Hans-Dietrich Genscher, held discussions with Shevardnadze to reach a compromise. On September 10, Shevardnadze announced that the two countries had reached an agreement of a German contribution of 12 billion *deutschemarks*.[56] In addition, he noted that the "grand treaty" between the FRG and the USSR was ready to sign.[57]

The final round of the talks addressed the remaining issues, in particular limits on the presence of non-German NATO troops, which could not be based in eastern Germany, and the deployment of dual-purpose weapons systems in the former GDR even after the Soviet withdrawal.[58] The treaty was signed on September 12, 1990 by the foreign ministers. In addition to the previously-mentioned supplement, the treaty also contained a protocol governing NATO maneuvers on the territory of the GDR after 1994.[59]

The following day, Genscher and Shevardnadze initialed the bilateral Comprehensive Treaty on Good-Neighborliness, Partnership, and Cooperation, which was to govern relations between an united Germany and the USSR. It was basically an "umbrella" agreement covering defense matters, economic issues, and financial assistance.[60] Specifically, both countries renounced the use of force, as well as any territorial claims against one another and pledged to "commit themselves to solving their disputes by peaceful means."[61] The treaty also established regular consultations, with summit meetings to be held once a year.

The actual implementation of these accords was somewhat anti-climatic. The unification treaty was approved and ratified by the FRG and the GDR in late September. The GDR had to formally leave the WTO, which involved an international protocol between the GDR and the WTO. As of October 3, the GDR would "no longer offer military assistance to the Warsaw Pact" and NVA representatives would withdraw from WTO institutions by October 2.[62] In addition, any WTO equipment, especially cipher equipment, in the GDR was to be turned over to the Soviet Army. Secret WTO documents were "to be either returned to the Soviets or destroyed" and the NVA was to take care that "the contents are not passed on to third countries."[63]

The Soviet parliament canceled the bilateral defense treaty with the GDR on the day of Germany's reunification.[64] The day before the formal unification, the *Bundeswehr* transferred 1,000 officers into NVA units to ensure a smooth transition of the East Germany military into an unified command structure.[65] On October 2, 1990, the People's Chamber formally dissolved itself and acceded to the Basic Law. At midnight, the GDR ceased to exist and its territory became the FRG *lander* (German states) of Brandenburg, Mecklenburg-Western Pomerania, Saxony, Saxony-Anhalt, and Thuringia, plus the city of Berlin (see the map overleaf).

The Eastern *Lander*

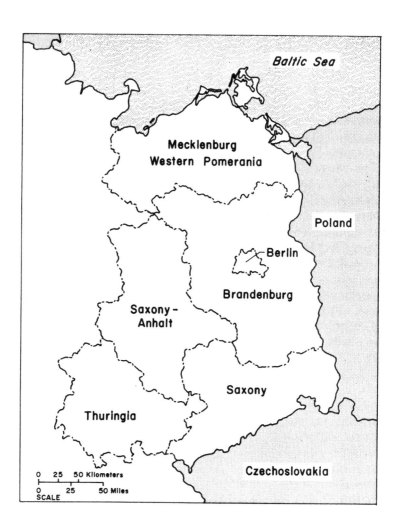

Source: Central Intelligence Agency, *Atlas of Eastern Europe, August 1990* (Washington, DC: USGPO, 1990), 22.

THE *BUNDESWEHR* EAST

The German government has tried to completely integrate the eastern Germans into the FRG, with mixed results. One of the more successful transitions, though, has been the takeover of the NVA by the *Bundeswehr*. Even before unification, the West German military had detailed plans for the unified command. When the GDR acceded to the Basic Law, the West German defense minister, Gerhard Stoltenberg, assumed command over the NVA, which temporarily became the Territorial Command East, also known as the *Bundeswehr* Command East.[66]

The eastern command was headed by Lieutenant General Jorg Schonbohm, who was previously the head of the *Bundeswehr*'s planning staff, with a staff of approximately eighty West German officers. The Territorial Command East was comprised of "two defense area commands" based in Leipzig and Neubrandenburg for the ground forces, while the former East German navy was commanded by the National Fleet Command in Glucksburg and the air forces were subordinate to the Air Force Command in Porz, both of which are located in western Germany.[67]

The principal mission of the six-month command was to deal "with the politically, organizationally, and psychologically difficult task of integrating the former NVA in the *Bundeswehr*."[68] Part of this integration involved the reduction of the eastern forces. Although the East Germans had reduced the NVA to less than 100,000 men before unification, the West Germans intended to reduce the Territorial Command to around 50,000. In addition, the former East German border guards would eventually be disbanded, although some of them would continue to clear the mines along the former inner-German border.[69]

A secondary purpose of the Territorial Command was to liaison with the WGF and to coordinate their withdrawal. Schonbohm met with Snetkov shortly after assuming command of the *Bundeswehr* East. The two commanders discussed the "limited stay and the final withdrawal of Soviet troops from Germany" and reaffirmed both countries' commitments under the recent treaties.[70] Schonbohm also appointed Major General Hartmut Fortsch as the head of the German liaison command with the Soviet forces in Germany.

The German liaison office was to represent German interests to the WGF and oversee the withdrawal.[71] In addition, the federal Center for *Bundeswehr* Verification Tasks, which was established to oversee German compliance with the Conventional Forces in Europe (CFE) Treaty, has an eastern branch office in the city of Strausberg. The Strausberg office, which was formerly the verification center for the NVA, carries out "all verification and inspection tasks" relating to the CFE Treaty in the eastern *lander*, including those that related to the WGF.[72]

At least none of this was completely new for the Soviets, since the Western allies previously had the right to inspect military facilities in Germany and the East Germans could address problems with the Soviets in the joint USSR–GDR commission.[73] The NVA, on the other hand, was "consigned to history"[74] and many servicemen lost their jobs. The remaining troops even had to wear *Bundeswehr* uniforms, as soon as the required number were available.[75] The largely surplus NVA equipment was frequently mothballed, although both Hungary and Czechoslovakia would later express interest in buying the former East German equipment.[76]

As noted, the Territorial Command was only in place for six months. After March 1991, the eastern German units were integrated into the *Bundeswehr* proper, although they were not were not initially assigned to NATO as called for in the 2 + 4 Treaty. An army command, composed of two military districts, was established in Potsdam for the ground troops, with an air force division headquartered in Eggersdorf and a navy section based in Rostock.[77] The number of former NVA personnel remained at 50,000, with half of these being professionals and the other half conscripts.[78]

Of course, the former NVA was not the only institution undergoing changes. The rest of the *Bundeswehr* was also being reduced in accordance with the 2 + 4 and the CFE treaties, while NATO was beginning a major revision of its strategy. The major change was the absence of "an enemy image."[79] The USSR was no longer seen as the likely aggressor, although it was considered to be unstable. Consequently, NATO discarded its forward defense strategy, which was largely intended to defend West Germany, and instead sought a defense in depth of NATO territory.

THE WGF AND GERMANY

One of the carryovers of the Cold War, however, was the WGF, which was ironically now stationed in a NATO country. Although economic questions dominated German–Soviet, and continue to do so for German–Russian, relations, the WGF was also a central issue between the two countries. The payments for the maintenance and withdrawal of the WGF, after all, accounted for much of the German assistance to Moscow.

With the dissolution of the WTO, the completed withdrawals from Hungary and Czechoslovakia, and the then-ongoing withdrawal from Poland, the WGF was increasingly isolated. Both the Soviet and German leadership recognized this, and Genscher promised to visit the Soviet troops soon after the signing of the 2 + 4 Treaty. The two countries signed a Treaty on the Conditions of the Temporary Presence and the Terms of the Planned Withdrawal on October 12, 1990, which codified the Gorbachev–Kohl agreement.[80] For their part, the Germans accepted the continued deployment and stretched-out withdrawal as "a confidence-building measure between the two states."[81]

It was an expensive measure, though. It was estimated that prior to unification, East Germany provided services and materials worth 700 million *ostmarks* a year to the WGF. The FRG had to assume these obligations after the currency union, which meant that the Soviet troops in Germany were now receiving *deutschemarks*.[82] All of the costs were part of the German assistance to the USSR. Since the WGF personnel were paid in German currency, some of these expenses were returned to the local economy.

Economics also dominated the WGF's "limited stay" in Germany. As the withdrawal progressed, housing for the soldiers and personnel of the WGF in USSR, and later in the Russian Federation, became more problematical. The German government, as part of the troop accord, was to provide money to build housing for the returnees. In 1991, for example, they allocated 7.8 million *deutschemarks* for this purpose.[83] The WGF command arranged with the Russian government to buy these apartments by earning money in Germany.[84]

One way the Western command relied on to make money was to sell advertising space on the fences of WGF bases. The Germans, however, accused the Soviet troops of selling surplus weapons in eastern Germany. This accusation was denied by the WGF commander.[85] It was also claimed that the Soviet forces maintained illegal stocks of chemical weapons in the country, which was also denied, but would strain German-Soviet relations nevertheless.[86] A secret trip by Yazov to the WGF in March 1991 added to tensions between the two countries over the presence of the Soviet troops.[87] The environmental costs of the Soviet troops would also increasingly become an issue between the two governments. The Germans claimed that WGF damaged the environment in the former GDR, primarily through vehicle maintenance, training, and base construction. In exchange for not charging the WGF for the necessary cleanup, they proposed a swap for the WGF property. The WGF command, however, instituted an environmental clean up, removing fuel and lubricants, filling in shelters, and repairing the soil damage.[88] In addition, the easterners were now free to complain about the noise and traffic created by the Soviet soldiers.

The environmental consequences were only one of the negative aspects of the continued deployment that soured relations between the Soviet troops and local residents. For a while after the overthrow of Honecker, East Germans generally looked favorably on the WGF because they had not intervened against the demonstrators. Even before the unification, however, the goodwill had worn off and the East Germans now wanted the Soviets out. Soviet barracks were shot at and soldiers beaten up.[89] In at least one case, a WGF soldier was murdered while off duty in Leipzig.[90]

Incidents aimed at the Soviet troops would increase throughout 1990 and afterwards. A monument and Soviet graves in Treptow Park in West Berlin were defaced by neo-Nazis in early 1990.[91] As noted, the Soviets considered such incidents important enough to include them in the 2 + 4 talks. The governments of the FRG and the GDR sent a diplomatic note to the other participants stating that such memorials would be protected under German law.[92] Thefts or attempted thefts of Soviet property also occurred as the withdrawal continued.

The conditions in Germany and the thoughts of worse conditions in the USSR led some WGF personnel to desert or seek political asylum. In September 1990, it was reported that 100 soldiers had deserted the WGF for West Germany that month alone and that the WGF command had issued an order to shoot at deserters.[93] The Soviets initially denied such reports, but Burlakov, the final commander-in-chief, would later admit that there had been some instances of desertion in the early stages of the withdrawal.[94]

The state of relations between the WGF and their German "hosts" were such that some Soviets began to question the speed of the withdrawal. Vyacheslav Dashichev, a government advisor on German affairs, had proposed a faster withdrawal even before unification, noting that there was no "point for our troops to stay in Germany," and that maintaining them was too expensive.[95] It was a sentiment that many people shared.

FAREWELL, GERMANY

The Soviets' strategic position in Eastern Europe had almost completely dissipated as they withdrew their Groups of Forces and many of the former WTO states sought to reorient themselves more to the West. Unlike most of the major breakups of hegemonic realms, the dissolution of the Soviet "empire" in Eastern Europe was largely peaceful. The USSR was not forced out by war but rather gave up its position, due to "Gorbachev's courageous policy of 'perestroyka' and the 'new thinking'" in Moscow.[96]

Whatever the reason, however, the Soviets were once again going east instead of heading west. The withdrawal of the WGF, as well as Soviet policy towards Eastern Europe, would increasingly become an issue in Soviet domestic politics as hard-line communists questioned the reorientation toward the West, while at the same time several nationalities were pushing for greater independence within or outright secession from the USSR. Like the German troops on the Eastern front in World War II, the Soviets themselves were now facing the possibility of:

Nema pivo, nema vino
Do Svidaniya, Ukraina

No more beer, no more wine. Goodbye, Ukraine.[97] For the troops of the WGF, much the same could be said about Germany.

6 Domestic Politics and the WGF

When sorrows come, they come not single spies/But in battalions
 – William Shakespeare, *Hamlet*, Act IV, scene v

With most of the major international problems relating to the WGF having been more or less solved, the principal focus of the withdrawal turned to domestic issues within the USSR. The returning troops came back to a very different country than even just a few years ago. Severe economic and nationality problems gripped the USSR, while new groups voiced their demands for change. These calls were from every part of the political spectrum, from even more radical reformers to hard-line communists and nationalists who were seeking to block the more liberal aspects of Gorbachev's reforms.

As noted, Gorbachev viewed his reforms as a means of achieving a socialist renewal. By the late 1980s, however, they had run into problems and were not stopping, and very likely accelerated, the relative loss of Soviet power. As for the WGF, and the Soviets' other European commands, the withdrawals symbolized the USSR's loss of hegemony over the region.

This chapter, then, looks at the domestic aspects of the withdrawal. It will deal with Moscow's reactions to the events in Eastern Europe, the logistics and politics of the withdrawal, the transfer of the command to first the Joint Armed Forces of the Commonwealth of Independent States (CIS) and then to the Russian Army, and the role of the WGF in Russian defense plans.

THE END OF THE EMPIRE

As the Soviet pullout from the region continued, the USSR tried to adapt to the loss of its hegemonic position. Even the

leaders of other countries noted the need not to make the
withdrawals difficult for the Soviets, so as not to weaken
Gorbachev's domestic position.[1] On the other hand, Czechoslovakia, Hungary, and Poland continued to pressure the
USSR to complete the withdrawals; while at the same time
the Soviets' European economic and military organizations
began to wither away.

In both Czechoslovakia and Hungary, the Soviets proceeded to withdraw units of the Central Group of Forces
(CGF) and the Southern Group of Forces (SGF), respectively.
They had agreed to somewhat tight schedules for these
withdrawals, as the two groups were relatively small in size
and both Czechoslovakia and Hungary bordered the USSR.
In both instances, the Soviets generally relied on rail transport
for the withdrawals. Throughout 1990, Soviet units left the
two countries in a sort of leapfrog manner, with one or two
units being pulled out, to be followed by other units.[2]

While the withdrawal of the Central and Southern forces
continued, economic and environmental concerns surfaced in
Czechoslovakia and Hungary, just as they had in eastern
Germany. The Czechoslovak and Hungarian governments
claimed that the Soviet forces had damaged the environment,
while the Soviets maintained that the buildings they were
vacating were being undervalued by the two countries. In
Hungary, the government would propose an exchange of the
Soviet property for the cleanup costs. Moscow initially
refused, as it claimed that the Soviet bases were worth fifty
billion *forints*.[3]

The Czechoslovaks had the same problem with a property
settlement, as the Soviets claimed their property in Czechoslovakia was worth 4,000 to 5,000 million *krone*.[4] The two
governments' estimates were about one-fifth of the Soviet
estimates. Eventually, the CIS states, and in particular Russia,
acting as the successors to the USSR, would eventually accept
the "zero option."[5] Although many of the environmental
problems were still present, the bilateral issues were at least
officially settled by the time the troops were out. The same
thing could not have been said for relations between the CGF

and local Czechoslovak officials, however. In one case, after authorities in the town of Frenstat "ordered" them to clean up their base, the Soviet troops reportedly destroyed their barracks and looted the town.[6]

For the other Eastern European countries with Groups of Forces, Frenstat represented the worst-case scenario of the Soviet retreat.[7] Overall, the withdrawals did not normally have open confrontations. Hungary and Czechoslovakia wanted the Soviet troops out and, like the Germans, were more than willing to agree to anything to get them out. The withdrawals did improve the general relations between the USSR and the two countries, though. Soviet officials noted that the ending of the CGF and SGF could provide the basis for building new relationships with the two states.[8]

The two Soviet commands were dissolved within two days of one another. The last units of the SGF left Hungary on June 19, 1991, while the CGF troops were out of Czechoslovakia by June 21, 1991.[9] General Matvey Burlakov was appointed the commander of the SGF and charged with organizing its withdrawal. Before the completion of the withdrawal, however, he was transferred to the WGF in December 1990 to oversee its withdrawal.[10] He would be the WGF's last commander-in-chief.

The Czechoslovakian and Hungarian withdrawals, unlike the withdrawal of the WGF, were undertaken and completed before the dissolution of the USSR. Consequently, units of the two commands were transferred back to several locations within the USSR without any concern about the future. Many of these forces were sent to the Ukraine, the Soviet republic which bordered the two countries, as were some of the WGF units.

By 1991, the Polish government decided that it too wanted the Soviet units out and began pressing for the withdrawal of the NGF and, as had Czechoslovakia, placed stringent conditions on the use of railroads to withdraw the WGF. The Soviets eventually agreed to withdraw the troops, but wanted to keep at least non-combat units in Poland as long as possible while the WGF was still in Germany.[11] As in

Czechoslovakia and Hungary, both sides agreed on a schedule for the withdrawal with the last combat units to be pulled out by November 15, 1992.[12]

In addition to the withdrawals of the Groups of Forces, the Soviet-led regional organizations, CEMA and the WTO, also had begun to outlive their usefulness. Many of the members of the WTO had wanted to unilaterally withdraw from the organization as early as 1990, but a formal dissolution was put off until later.[13] Instead, the military aspects of the WTO were to be minimized as it was "to be gradually converted into a political community based on treaties."[14] As noted, East Germany had left the pact, with the approval of the other members, before the reunification.

The WTO did not outlive East Germany by very long, however. As the new governments of Eastern Europe introduced more reforms, including military reforms, they would increasingly look to Western Europe and NATO for security guarantees. Several of the members, in particular Czechoslovakia, Hungary, and Poland, openly talked of joining NATO.[15] As the Soviets became increasingly concerned with domestic problems, they agreed to allow the Warsaw Pact organization to lapse in 1991. Soon afterwards, NATO established the North Atlantic Co-operation Council to coordinate ties with many of the former WTO states and the countries that emerged from the dissolution of the USSR.

CEMA did not make it much further, either. As the Eastern European countries adopted market economies, and the USSR moved towards one, an international organization based on coordinating planned economies had largely become obsolete. It too was dissolved, as the members sought to reintegrate themselves in the world economy. CEMA had become "a dinosaur trying to find a place in the world which has no need of dinosaurs."[16] Neither of the Soviets' multilateral control mechanisms for keeping Eastern Europe in line survived new thinking.

At the same time, new thinking itself was being called into question in the USSR. Anti-reformers, including hard-line communists and Russian nationalists, attacked Gorbachev's domestic and foreign policies in the Soviet parliament. In general, the people who opposed Gorbachev's reforms viewed *perestroika* as a failure and *glasnost* was held to be a dangerous precedent. Gorbachev's attempts to reform Soviet society was only leading to chaos. In foreign affairs, Gorbachev's new thinking, and especially the pro-Western outlook, was viewed as too one-sided as the USSR was seen as giving up too much unilaterally.

The acceptance of non-socialist regimes in Eastern Europe was one of the changes that hard-liners used to attack Gorbachev and Shevardnadze. The more extreme nationalists viewed the events of 1989 as giving up the gains of World War II, while other critics, even though they accepted the need to eventually withdraw, thought that Gorbachev had moved too fast and without getting enough concessions from the West.[17] Both Gorbachev and Shevardnadze defended their actions before the parliament, with Gorbachev noting "what were we supposed to do? Should we have used axes and tanks and tried to teach them another lesson in how to live?"[18]

Soviet policy towards Eastern Europe survived the legislative questioning, although Shevardnadze resigned as foreign minister, in part because of the increasingly personal nature of the attacks, in December 1990. Given that the USSR had signed international agreements concerning Eastern Europe there was very little the hard-liners could have done, aside from changing the government. For the USSR to intervene yet again would have crossed out "everything to do with *perestroyka* and democratization."[19] The Soviet withdrawals would continue.

LOGISTICAL CONCERNS

The withdrawal of the WGF was one of the most complex peacetime military operations in history. It involved not only moving almost half-a-million personnel and their associated equipment, but also liquidating a fifty-year presence in a foreign land. In addition, the withdrawal occurred on top of the related withdrawals from other former-WTO countries. It is not surprising, therefore, that logistical problems dominated the withdrawal process.

During their "limited stay," the WGF had, as the other Soviet groups had done in Czechoslovakia, Hungary, and Poland, built up extensive facilities to provide support for the units. In the eastern German *land* of Brandenburg, for example, the WGF had 324 bases located on a total of 120,000 hectares.[20] This region had about 35 percent of the Soviet forces in eastern Germany and almost half the territory, as well as most of the training areas in the former GDR.[21] Eventually, the Russian government formed a commission to deal with various property issues, both in Germany and in Russia.[22]

As noted, the Soviets either tried to return these areas to a more natural state or improve the structures before they left. The bigger headaches were in getting the troops to the USSR and housing them when they got there. The Soviets would have preferred to transport the WGF by train as it had done in the withdrawals of the CGF and SGF, but both the Czechoslovak and Polish governments wanted the Soviets to pay "a vast sum for each freight car" and repair any damage incurred by the transshipment.[23]

Since the USSR was facing severe economic problems, the Soviets could not afford these conditions and decided to ship the bulk of the equipment out by sea from eastern German ports to either the Kaliningrad *oblast* (region) of the USSR, Klaipeda in the Lithuanian republic, or Leningrad,[24] where it was unloaded and forwarded to a more permanent location. WGF units would literally pack up their bases, either put the equipment of German railcars or use the roads, and send it to one of three German ports: Mukran, Rostock or Wismar.[25]

This process "turned out to be fraught with problems."[26] To begin with, the Soviets would have to close off areas where loading or unloading was taking place,[27] which required coordination with local officials. Once they reached their destination, Soviet property was subject to theft in the relatively uncontrolled ports. In response, the Soviets organized "operational groups" to guard the equipment in the port areas.[28]

The sea-borne withdrawal allowed the Soviets to move almost all of the equipment and material and about forty percent of the soldiers, or about 34,000 pieces of equipment totalling 800,000 tonnes and 168,000 soldiers. The remainder of the WGF personnel, including all of the civilians, were flown out.[29] The Czechoslovaks and Poles would later change their minds and lower their prices, but the Soviets largely stuck with their "maritime 'maneuvers,'"[30] although some of the ammunition and vehicles were shipped by rail through Poland.[31]

At first, the Soviets would ship an entire unit back to the USSR and then disband it, posting the personnel to other units. By 1992, however, the WGF assumed the responsibility for disbanding units and notifying people of new assignments while they were still in Germany.[32] Not that all of them had new assignments. The force reductions meant that there were fewer command slots opening up in the Soviet Army, and the coming breakup of the USSR and the subsequent establishment of national armies, led to even further reductions in the size of the military.

The scale of the withdrawal was staggering. At one point, the WGF was running sixty railway trains a day to the German ports.[33] By comparison, the Americans withdrew sixty battalions from Germany in 1991, the British one, and the French ten. The WGF alone withdrew 430, admittedly smaller, battalions that same year.[34] Unlike the others, however, the Soviet troops almost literally had no place to go. The earlier withdrawals and the existence of a housing shortage in the USSR meant that some of the returnees had no where to live.

As noted, the German government was required by treaty to help build housing for the WGF personnel. The FRG government did allocate funds to help construct apartments and German firms helped build some of these.[35] Some of these were in the Russian Soviet Federative Socialist Republic, while others were in the Ukraine. As mentioned, the WGF used funds it had earned in Germany to help officers buy these apartments.[36] All of these efforts would fall short of providing everyone with a place, however. Some of the soldiers and their families were forced to live in tents in Kaliningrad, Moscow, and other cities.

The logistical problems, however, would soon be over-shadowed by political concerns as the reforms themselves were compromised as Gorbachev allied with hard-line elements in an attempt to maintain central control. The Soviet Army was generally considered to be one of the more hard-line groups, although many of the younger officers supported Gorbachev. As it turned out, the army itself was divided over the course of *perestroika*.

THE DEMOCRATIZATION OF THE WGF

Gorbachev's reforms were different from previous efforts in that they were applied to all aspects of Soviet society, including the military and the previously sacrosanct KGB. The military was one of the first institutions to undergo extensive personnel changes as Gorbachev retired many of the older Brezhnev appointees. In addition to this example of *perestroika*, the army was also subject to both *glasnost* and *demokratizatsiya*, in an effort to make the military more open and accountable.

The reforms radically changed the nature of Soviet civil–military relations. The basic division of labor for national security, with the CPSU determining the broad outlines and the army deciding how to implement the party's guidelines, began to break down as new actors, including civilian think-tanks and the Soviet legislature, made their interests known. In addition, Soviet defense policy was now under increased scrutiny by the media. By the late 1980s, the Soviet Army, like many other aspects of the Soviet system, had become openly politicized.

The inclusion of the military in the reform program led to an increasingly public debate between Gorbachev and Yazov, his defense minister. Yazov, who was selected to replace Sergey Sokolov following the Mathias Rust incident in 1987, when a young West German flew a Cessna into Red Square in

Moscow, openly supported the aims of *perestroika* but questioned the need for openness in the military. Gorbachev, who, as chairman of the Defense Council, and the Supreme Commander-in-Chief of the Soviet Army, won out, however. It was the first public disagreement between the two men, but not the last.

Like most Soviet organizations, the army had a varied record of success in implementing the reforms. The WGF was no exception, as it sought to keep up with the changes in Soviet society. From the WGF command's point of view, the most important component of the reforms was the restructuring. In theory, *perestroika* could have led to a more capable and better supplied army, in which "the level of troops' operational-tactical training, arms, and technical equipment reliably ensures their fulfillment of all their tasks."[37] In reality, however, the restructuring of the WGF was largely decided by Gorbachev's unilateral reductions and the subsequent withdrawal. After 1994, there wouldn't be a WGF to restructure.

Questions about democracy and openness in the command proved to be more contentious. At a party conference in the unit, delegates complained about the social problems of WGF personnel, the defense cutbacks, and continued reliance on old, administrative command methods in party work.[38] Lev Zaykov, the *Politburo* member in charge of the defense industry, attended the 1990 conference and noted deficiencies in both the unit's combat readiness and in its political training,[39] in particular the problems relating to maintaining morale in "a non-socialist environment."[40] He also explained to the delegates the steps the CPSU leadership was taking in the country as a whole.

At least one soldier in the WGF took the reforms to heart, as a reform-minded officer decided to challenge Snetkov, then the commander-in-chief, for the WGF's seat, based in the city of Yaroslavl in the USSR, in the Congress of People's Deputies in 1989. In a highly publicized election, Lieutenant Colonel Viktor Podziruk ran on an electoral platform of military reform, while Snetkov stressed a more traditional approach to defence issues. Podziruk largely had to make do with volunteers, including the Yaroslaval Popular Front, in

his effort, while Snetkov had the official backing of the army
and the party.[41] Despite the odds, Podziruk won the election
and represented the WGF in the Soviet legislature. In many
ways, this election symbolized the debate over reform in the
USSR.

THE AUGUST COUP

In addition to foreign policy concerns, the hard-liners also
questioned the effects of Gorbachev's policies within the
USSR. Principally, they felt that the moves towards a market
economy and increased autonomy for the republics were
breaking the power of the central organs. They managed to
water-down the Shatalin Plan and would later attempt to
transfer much of the president's powers to the prime minister,
Valentin Pavlov. After this attempted "coup" in January
1991, Gorbachev supported, or was forced to support, a
strong central government.

The Soviet Army was increasingly used to crack down
against independence efforts by nationalists in many of the
republics. The most publicized conflict came when Alpha
Group, a KGB special forces unit, seized control of the
Vilnius television tower in January 1991. In the political
aftermath of the assault, Gorbachev would eventually enter
into negotiations with republican leaders on a new Union
treaty, which would give more power to the republics. Known
as the Novo-Ogarev, or the Nine-plus-One, agreement, it
would have given the republics more autonomy, including
control over their finances, and a reduced role for the central
government.

The Union Treaty, which was scheduled to be signed on
August 20, 1991, proved to be the final straw for the hard-
liners. On August 19, an Emergency Committee for the State
of the Emergency, composed of government and party
officials, placed Gorbachev under house arrest in his retreat
in the Crimea and named the Soviet vice-president, Gennady
Yaneyev, as acting president. The committee declared a state

of emergency throughout the country and deployed army units to enforce the decree.

The Soviet people, at least in Moscow and other major cities, refused to accept the emergency decree quietly and came out in large numbers to protest about the committee's seizure of power. Muscovites in particular came out to protect the Russian parliament building, known as the "White House," from an assault like the one in Lithuania. Some Soviet army units refused to obey the committee's orders and others would even "defect" to the opposition, which was led by the Russian president, Boris Yeltsin.

The coup began to unravel when the leaders backed down from using force against the opposition groups. Vladimir Kruychkov, the chairman of the KGB and the purported leader of the coup, flew to the Crimea to try to get Gorbachev's support, but was instead arrested, as were most of the other plotters. Gorbachev flew back to Moscow to resume his position, but quickly found that things had changed. Yeltsin, who had been popularly elected as president of the Russian federation in June, was now in a position to dictate terms to Gorbachev. The reform effort had a new standard-bearer.

The attempted coup never directly affected the WGF or its withdrawal. Burlakov noted that the state of emergency decree only applied to "the military areas within the USSR" and consequently he did not institute any different measures during the coup.[42] Similarly, the withdrawal was governed by the Soviet–German troop accord and the 2 + 4 Treaty, so, even if they had been successful, the committee would have been bound by the international agreements or would have to abrogate them, which was highly unlikely. During the coup attempt, Burlakov openly stated that the withdrawal would continue, regardless of the events in Moscow.[43]

Nevertheless, the three days in August were tense for the concerned parties, especially in the West. The German government monitored the situation, both in Moscow and in eastern Germany, but found that the WGF soldiers "stood the test."[44] The other major worry for the Germans was the loyalty of the former NVA soldiers in the *Bundeswehr*. They did not give their commanders any cause for concern, however, since they "acted loyally in the critical days," demonstrating the effectiveness of the integration.[45]

The failed coup did, however, dramatically change the domestic political situation and the future of the WGF. Yeltsin would begin to institute even more radical reforms than Gorbachev ever had. Instead of a Soviet socialist renewal, he sought to dismantle communism in Russia. Yeltsin also wanted to decentralize power to the republics and when Ukrainians voted overwhelmingly in favor of independence, he agreed to the establishment of a new confederation, the Commonwealth of Independent States, with the leaders of Belarus and Ukraine on December 8, 1991. The rest of the other Soviet republics, except for Azerbaijan, the Baltic states and Georgia, joined the CIS two weeks later.

The USSR was formally dissolved in December 1991 and Gorbachev retired from public service. The new Commonwealth also established a Joint Armed Forces of the CIS, with the former head of the Soviet Air Force, Yevegeny Shaposnikov, as its head. The WGF, along with the rest of the Soviet Army, was taken over by the new command.

THE CIS INTERREGNUM

The changes in Moscow did not immediately affect the WGF all that much. The joint command was still headquartered in Moscow and the WGF continued to withdraw, but now onto formerly Soviet territory. As many of the former republics went about building their own armies, however, units of the WGF were increasingly sent to the Russian Republic as a prelude to the establishment of a Russian military. The Joint Armed Forces of the CIS consisted of two commands, strategic forces and ground forces. The strategic forces contained the Strategic Rocket Forces, air units, the Airborne Troops, and naval forces. It was originally agreed by the CIS signatories that these forces would remain under central control in Moscow, although the other members would retain a veto over the use of nuclear weapons. The conventional forces would have sort of a dual allegiance, based on where they were stationed.

Since the WGF was outside CIS territory, it had a somewhat nebulous status until a unit was actually brought back. The dissolution of the USSR, however, meant that units were increasingly left in the Kaliningrad *oblast* instead of being transferred to another base. Kaliningrad, formerly Konigsberg, the capital of East Prussia when it was German territory, was subordinate to the Leningrad Military District, which encompassed the area around Leningrad (shortly to be Saint Petersburg again), Karelia and the Kola peninsula and was entirely within the Russian Republic.

The change to leaving WGF units in Kaliningrad following their withdrawal from Germany meant that the *oblast* had one of the highest concentrations of military firepower in the world. There was little else in the region aside from military units, except for largely ethnic Russians, who had resettled there after the war.[46] It also meant that the WGF was moving from one part of Germany to a former part, since the region had been the home of the Prussian *junkers* before its post-World War II dismemberment.

The other short-term consequence of the collapse of the USSR for the WGF had to do with the role of the Communist party within the command. Even before the coup attempt, Yeltsin had banned CPSU activity in army units and the KGB on Russian territory. Now, even WGF units still in eastern Germany began to disband communist organizations within their ranks.[47] The activities of primary party organization, the smallest units of the CPSU, were stopped and the political officers ceased their indoctrination programs.

The CIS never quite developed as some of its members had hoped, however. Ukrainian officials, wary of close ties with the Russians, preferred that the organization remain "soft," while the former Central Asian republics wanted the CIS to promote a higher level of integration among the new states, especially on economic and defense issues. By and large, the Russian government also wanted to retain the close ties established by the Soviets and showed little signs of wanting to build their own army. Events overtook these desires, however, and in March 1992, Yeltsin authorized the formation of a Russian Ministry of Defense.[48]

THE RE-ESTABLISHMENT OF THE RUSSIAN ARMY

When Yeltsin was first elected chairman of the Russian parliament in 1990, he and his supporters intentionally set out to use the Russian Federation to weaken the power of the central government. First, however, they had to establish or create Russian, as opposed to Soviet, organizations, since the Soviets never really developed Russian institutions.[49] When the failed coup accelerated the collapse of the USSR, the Russian government inherited some, but not all, of the Soviet bureaucracies.

One bureaucracy they did not directly take over was the military. As noted, they first attempted to maintain an united armed forces through the CIS. As many of the other former republics, especially Ukraine, moved to create their own armies, Yeltsin re-established the Russian Army on May 7, 1992. General Pavel Grachev, the former commander of the Airborne Troops who had sided with Yeltsin during the abortive 1991 coup, was named defense minister, with General Boris Gromov, the last Soviet commander in Afghanistan, and Andrey Kokoshin, a civilian defense expert, as first deputy ministers.

The new high command faced a daunting task. Budget problems made it difficult to pay for any sort of military, never mind one suited to a former superpower, desertion rates were high, morale throughout the army was low, and operational readiness was also low as many units had reduced or non-existent training schedules. To make matters worse, many of the units of the former Soviet Army on Russian territory were below-standard mobilization units. To address these deficiencies, the Russian Army introduced a reform program to bring the new army up to modern-day standards.

The Soviets had previously begun far-ranging reforms brought about by the performance of the Soviet military in Afghanistan, which demonstrated the shortcomings of an overcentralized command structure and a reliance on a conscript force, and the overwhelming American success against the largely Soviet-modelled Iraqi Army in the Gulf War. Both of these conflicts revealed the weaknesses of Soviet military thinking in relation to present-day warfare.

The fundamental change in the Russian Army, doctrinal reform, followed from the late Soviet revisions under reasonable sufficiency. The military would not be configured to carry out offensive operations, but rather it would be used to deter attacks on the Russian Federation.[50] The Russians, however, went further, and recognized that most of the possible threats were what are referred to as low-intensity conflicts. The Russian Army would have to be more flexible and mobile to deal with small wars on the periphery of the country.[51]

This new doctrine relies heavily on the former Soviet special forces, which included the airborne forces, naval infantry and *spetsnaz* units, to act as a central reserve to respond to a crisis.[52] A new service, *Mobilnyye Sily Rossii* (the Russian Mobile Force) was established in 1992 to coordinate and integrate many of the special units under one command. The doctrine also called for the development of reserve territorial units to be called up in the case of an attack and the reorganization the former Soviet ground forces into ground defense forces.

The ground defense forces are to be reconfigured to be able to conduct a mobile defense,[53] which involves temporarily surrendering territory while an attacker overextends himself and then launching a counterattack. This aspect of the Russian doctrine is almost a direct carryover from the later conceptions of reasonable sufficiency. A mobile defense, however, requires a largely decentralized command system and a high degree of initiative on the part of both the officers and soldiers. As a result, the Russians continued and expanded on the Soviets' introduction of contract service into an otherwise conscript force.

The ground defense forces have one of the most important roles in the new Russian strategy. A central concept of a mobile defense is the "fixing force," which attempts to hold the attacking units until reinforcements can redress the balance and launch a counterattack.[54] Even though the strategy ultimately relies on airpower and airmobile units to defeat an invader, the ground defense forces, which would serve as the fixing force, are literally the units on the front lines. Not surprisingly then, the WGF, as "the most powerful and battleworthy grouping" of the Russian units, was to form the core of the ground defense forces.[55]

The two remaining groups of forces in Eastern Europe, the NGF and WGF, were both subordinated to the Russian Federation even before the Russian Army was reestablished.[56] To some extent, the WGF's subordination to the Russian command, even though it was outside CIS territory, represented compensation to the Russians for the previous Soviet re-deployments which left many of the more capable units in the now independent Belarus and Ukraine. At any rate, only the Ukrainian government protested the Russian assumption of command, as it wanted its share of the former Soviet property and its assigned contingent of troops.[57]

Since it was planned for the WGF to form the basis of the new Russian ground troops, the government began to rethink its policy of disbanding withdrawn units from the WGF. Instead, units were transferred intact to Kaliningrad, from where they would now be posted to one of the other Russian military districts. Since the WGF command was to be dissolved upon completion of the withdrawal, the units were equally distributed to all the military districts in the country.[58]

In theory, this plan gave each military district front-rank units, while the non-WGF units were built up to Category A standards. In reality, there were serious questions about the capabilities of the WGF units. Even though it had been the elite strike force of the Soviet Army, by the early 1990s, the effects of the withdrawal meant that its potential had been heavily reduced. According to a defector, it was not capable of serious combat, the soldiers had serious morale problems, and the officers were preoccupied with their own careers.[59]

Before its transfer to the Russian Army, the command was:

on the verge of ruin. Anything that can be unscrewed and removed is stolen. One commission follows another. And you are always to blame, you are always threatened with arrest – either because of discipline of because of the disappearance of valuables, under the penalty of legal proceedings.[60]

Furthermore, after the currency union in June 1990, the soldiers were paid in *deutschemarks*, which is a hard currency and generally unavailable to Soviet citizens. The German currency quickly dominated life in the WGF and some officers reportedly would do anything to stay in eastern Germany to continue to receive the hard currency, which could be traded on the black market.[61] At the same time, reports of illegal weapons sales, including supposed offers of nuclear arms, by members of the WGF would continue.

One of the new tasks facing the Russian Army has been attempting to keep the peace in several of the former Soviet republics. Russian airborne units served as a peace-keeping force in South Ossetia in Georgia, as well as being part of the UN force in Croatia. The Russians have also begun to develop more specialized peace-keeping forces. One of these will be the 27th Guards Motor-rifle Division, which underwent joint training with an American unit at the Totskoye training ground in Russia. The 27th Guards unit was, appropriately enough, part of the 8th Guards Army of the WGF.[62]

THE POLITICS OF DEFENSE

As Yeltsin and his supporters introduced western-style reforms in Russia, they too ran into opposition. The Congress of People's Deputies, a holdover from the Gorbachev era, was dominated by former communists and Russian nationalists who joined together to fight the liberal policies of Yeltsin. In terms of domestic policies, the "Red–Brown alliance" wanted to end, or at least slow down, the privatization of former Soviet enterprises and weaken the powers of the Russian

presidency. In foreign affairs, they largely opposed the pro-
Western leanings of Yeltsin and his foreign minister, Andrey
Kozyrev.

Defense issues were not prominent in the struggle between
the reformers and the more reactionary elements. The Russian
Federation could barely afford to keep the units it had.
Nevertheless, the increased politicization of Russian life
continued to influence how defense policy was made in
general and the WGF specifically. The legislature, through the
Defense and Security Committee of the Supreme Soviet, kept
a close watch on defense issues in general and the withdrawal
of the WGF in particular. A legislative delegation visited the
WGF shortly after the reestablishment of the Russian Army
and supported the Defense Ministry's decision to discontinue
the disbandment of WGF units.[63]

As the struggle between the president and the congress
continued, Yeltsin proposed a referendum to break the
deadlock and the congress accepted the non-binding popular
vote. In the days before the April 1993 referendum, several
Russian Army officers, including Defense Minister Grachev,
Defense Ministry personnel, and commanders of the WGF,
were implicated in " 'illegal deals' involving former Soviet
military property in east Germany."[64] These initial charges
were later found to be unsubstantiated and were apparently an
unsuccessful election-eve ploy to discredit Yeltsin.

Reports of illegal sales of military property would continue
for the remainder of the command and even after the final
withdrawal. A 1993 investigation by the defense committee of
the Congress of People's Deputies did not find any evidence
but a journalist following the story was killed by a bomb in
October 1994. This incident was partially responsible for the
removal of Burlakov from his post-WGF position as a deputy
defense minister.

THE LAST WESTERNER

The actual withdrawal continued, largely on schedule, and
without any major incidents. By 1994, the only units

remaining were the 10th Guards Tank Division and the 47th Guards Tank Division of the 3rd Shock Army, plus two independent units, the 34th Artillery Division and the 6th Motor-rifle Brigade, and air units.[65] As with the other withdrawals of the groups of forces, combat units were pulled out first, leaving mostly administrative personnel. In both Czechoslovakia and Hungary, for example, the last persons to leave were the commanders of the groups, General Eduard Vorobyev of the CGF and Lieutenant General V. Shilov of the SGF.[66]

This was also the pattern of the Soviet withdrawal from Afghanistan, where the last man out was Gromov, the head of the 40th Army. After Gromov crossed the Termez bridge onto Soviet territory from Afghanistan on February 14, 1989, he "thought" a speech which he didn't voice and consequently no one heard. It was perhaps a fitting end to the Soviet involvement in Afghanistan. In Poland, however, the Russian troops were given an official farewell, which Yeltsin attended. The WGF was similarly given an elaborate send-off, although it was a separate ceremony from the Western Allies' withdrawal from Berlin.

Both Yeltsin and Kohl showed up to see the Russians leave "German soil."[67] The 6th Motor-rifle Brigade, or the Separate Berlin Order of Bogdan Khmelnitsky Motorized Guard's Brigade, detailed a special unit to participate in the official ceremonies, which included an impromptu conducting session by Yeltsin. These troops were the last Russian troops to leave Germany, arriving in Moscow on September 1, 1994. Even before the final withdrawal, Burlakov was promoted to deputy Defense Minister but, as noted above, he was released from that post a little over a month later when he was implicated in the alleged corruption of the WGF.

7   The Withdrawal and the End of the Cold War

O farewell honest soldier! Who hath reliev'd you?
    – William Shakespeare, *Hamlet*, Act 1, scene i

The pullout of the WGF marked the end of Soviet hegemony in Eastern Europe. Long before the withdrawal, which was the last of the Soviet withdrawals from Eastern Europe, was completed, the Soviets' European economic and military organizations and the USSR itself were dissolved. While the opening of the Berlin Wall was perhaps the most symbolic event of the long process of the Soviet retreat, the withdrawal of the Soviet troops from Eastern Europe both epitomized and exemplified this loss of hegemony.

The WGF wound up being at the center of the ending of the Cold War, which was inevitable given its pivotal role in the events and plans of the post-World War II period. The withdrawal also marked the nexus between these international events and domestic politics in the former USSR. The forces themselves, moreover, represent a measure of continuity, but also change, from the post-war period to the post-Cold War era as they carry out their new tasks in the Russian Federation.

This chapter, then, looks at the implications of the withdrawal for: post-Cold War international politics; Soviet, and Russian, relations with Germany; and the dissolution of the USSR. It also offers some concluding thoughts on the pullout.

THE END OF THE COLD WAR . . . AND WORLD WAR II

The Cold War, like any historical event, had many causes; yet it really came down to the clash of ideologies, between

123

liberalism in the west and communism in the east. Whatever the specific cause or whose fault it was, the Cold War ultimately came about because of the Soviet control of and the imposition of communism on the countries of Eastern Europe. The war was declared over in 1989 when, appropriately enough, the Soviets accepted political pluralism in the region.

When the Eastern European socialist regimes began to crumble in the fall of 1989, many people in the west viewed these events as a sign of the victory of western-style capitalism and democracy over state socialism. Yet, in retrospect, it was more an acquiescence by the Soviets than a defeat. The USSR had, as the logical, if unintended, consequence of new thinking, voluntarily given up their control over Eastern Europe. Despite the enormous problems facing the USSR in the late 1980s, there was no sign that Western policies, in particular the American strategy of containment, had forced the Soviets out of the region.

Indeed, many of the Soviet reformers noted how difficult it was to carry on with *glasnost* and *perestroika* while the United States continued with containment. Hard-liners in the *Politburo* used the American policy as justification for keeping the Stalinist command system in place, especially the high priority given to defense, and a confrontational foreign policy.[1] Rather, it was the recognition by the reformers that the system had to change, not because of international pressure but because of its inherent flaws, that led to the ending of the Cold War. This victory for reform was, however, largely the result of domestic politics within the USSR.

Gorbachev, Shevardnadze, and Aleksandr Yakovlev, Gorbachev's principal adviser on the reforms, may never had gotten the chance to fundamentally alter the USSR if it hadn't been for Khrushchev's earlier reform efforts. Despite a neo-Stalinist backlash during the Brezhnev years, the hopes of a more humane socialism continued, first with the dissident movement and then within the CPSU itself. In addition, the people who had grown up under Khrushchev, known as the "Thaw Generation,"[2] were beginning to replace the older, World War II generation in the government and the party. It was this combination of dissent and demographics that led to the changes in the USSR, including the shift in Soviet policy towards Eastern Europe and the eventual collapse of state socialism in the USSR.

Someone, however, had to have the courage to actually attempt to change things and, of course, that person was Gorbachev. In the final analysis, it was his new thinking that ended the Cold War. He was the one who decided that the Soviet people "can't go on living like this."[3] It was Gorbachev who let the other socialist regimes stand or fall on their own. He was, after all, the only General Secretary not to use force in Eastern Europe. While Gorbachev would ultimately become a prisoner of his reforms as far as Eastern Europe was concerned, in that he could have hardly intervened while at the same time talking about new political thinking, he still made the original decision to go ahead and change Soviet policies and society.

Perhaps the best historical analogy to the end of the Cold War was the end of the Thirty Years' War. Even after the Treaty of Westphalia gave the German principalities the right to choose their religious affiliation, France and Spain continued to fight for several years. Despite the near exhaustion of the two countries, they carried on their conflict "like two punch drunk fighters."[4] It was only when Britain entered the war on the side of France that the Spanish finally sought peace.[5]

By the end of the 1980s, the United States and the USSR were continuing the Cold War, even though neither of them could really afford to.[6] Unlike the Thirty Years' War, however, no third country entered the struggle to tip the balance. Instead it was the reform process that led the Soviets to throw in the towel first. By admitting that the Stalinist system needed to be changed, they also gave up their attempt at world hegemony and their control over Eastern Europe. In the case of the WTO states, at least, the Soviets knew what was going on, but "chose not to intervene."[7]

In doing so, new thinking also reoriented the USSR to the West to a degree unmatched in Soviet history. It was "a decisive break with old approaches and stereotypes,"[8] one that allowed for the partial reintegration of the USSR with the rest of the world. Soviet foreign policy was redirected away from the promotion of socialism, regardless of the cost, to the protection "by nonmilitary means the best external conditions for the country's economic development."[9] To a large extent, Yeltsin has continued with and expanded this orientation. Russia has moved towards the implementation of some of the principles of classical liberalism, including private property and popular consent, as well as the later American idea of federalism.

This reorientation had begun even before the dissolution of the USSR. As Yeltsin sought to build up Russian institutions, he and his supporters also turned their attention to foreign policy. Russia, as distinct from the USSR, would reject "a global strategy" and instead adopt "a rational-regional" approach.[10] The principal regional focus would be Europe, with the emphasis on Germany which, as a result of the changes brought about by new thinking, was now closer to Russia "in both the literal and the figurative sense."[11]

The German–Soviet rapprochement marked not just one part of the end of the Cold War, but also one of the final acts of World War II. The artificial division of German territory was finally addressed, again in large part due to the Soviets' new thinking, the wartime allies finally surrendered their formal obligations concerning Germany, and the withdrawal of most of the foreign troops on German soil was begun. The Americans, British and French reduced their military forces in Germany, while the Soviets, who had suffered more than any of the other major powers in the war, had decided to go home.

The withdrawal of the WGF marked the turning of "one of the last pages of the Second World War."[12] By giving up their effective occupation of eastern Germany, the Soviets were also giving up their security zone in Eastern Europe, which was by now of dubious military value. The doctrinal reforms associated with reasonable sufficiency had largely done away with the need for an offensive springboard. The defensive orientation now focused on safeguarding the USSR, and, after the collapse of the union, Russia.

By giving up the Stalinist command system, which was rationalized by Stalin as a means of preparation for the coming Second World War, the Soviets were making peace with the rest of the world. The world was no longer seen as divided into two camps, but was now viewed as being interdependent. Moreover, the USSR did not have a "special role" and the world would develop with or without it.[13] The enemy image of the capitalist West was replaced by an open invitation for foreign assistance and investment.

The Soviet search for absolute security was also replaced by a willingness to talk about a security partnership with the West. The USSR, despite its extensive ties with Iraq, supported the UN sanctions and military operations to force the Iraqis out of Kuwait. Russian President Yeltsin openly supported NATO's "Partnership for Peace" plan to engage the countries of Eastern Europe and the former USSR in bilateral arrangements for joint exercises, peacekeeping, and planning, which could ultimately lead to full membership, although Russia would also express concerns over an early expansion of NATO to Eastern Europe.

THE GERMAN SOLUTION

The Soviet disavowal of hegemony in Eastern Europe, the unification of Germany, and the withdrawal of the WGF also reflected a major change in the attitudes of the Soviets towards the German people. Germany and Russia, and then Germany and the USSR, had alternated between the extremes of close cooperation and outright conflict, as well as numerous stages in between, throughout their histories.

Strategically, if not ideologically, World War II was the latest in a series of German attacks on Russia. The division of Germany into two separate states, each reflecting a different social system, was essentially Stalin's solution to what has been termed the German problem, that is German aggression, in Europe. If Stalin could not control all of Germany, then he would accept control over part of it, since a divided Germany would not represent so much of a threat. Furthermore, the Red Army would be in the heart of Europe and hence in a position to prevent another attack by the Western countries, like the Allied intervention in the Russian Civil War.

The major flaw of the post-war division of Germany, and of Europe as a whole, was that, in addition to adding to Cold War tensions, it created the problem of German unification. As the East German revolution of 1989 demonstrated, the nationalistic yearnings for unification managed to outlast forty years of socialist internationalism. By supporting the East German reformers against Honecker and then by accepting the inevitable reunification of Germany, Gorbachev overturned one of the cornerstones of Soviet post-war foreign policy. In effect, he opted for a German solution, both internationally and within the USSR.

A united Germany would become the center of the "Common European Home," which was hardly anything new since the Germans had long held the view of their country as *mitteleuropa* (the middle of Europe). Since West Germany had the largest economy in Western Europe, a reunified Germany, with an domestic market of eighty million people, would also, at least in theory, be the economic powerhouse of the continent. Germany, which had a long history of economic ties with the countries of Central and Eastern Europe, could also assume greater responsibility for the former WTO states.

Gorbachev also wanted German assistance for *perestroika*. West Germany was already the largest trading partner of the USSR, a situation that predated even detente. Unification should have provided "the USSR a chance for long term cooperation with a politically stable and economically advanced country in the center of Europe."[14] It was also the natural western partner to help the Soviets over their economic problems and to integrate the Soviet economy with the world market. In addition to the outright support for the WGF, the West German government also underwrote loans from West German banks to the USSR and sent advisors to help in the transition to a market economy.[15]

West German–Soviet relations had markedly improved from the time when Kohl compared Gorbachev to Josef Goebbels, the Nazi Minister of Propaganda. The collapse of socialism in East Germany and Soviet acceptance of unification only moved the two states closer. As the USSR implemented more western-style reforms, the more it had in common with Germany as well as the complimentary nature of the two economies. Germany had capital and finished products, while the USSR had raw materials and an export market.

The improved relations, signified by the German–Soviet treaty, continued even after the dissolution of the USSR. As noted, the Russian government had started to establish relations with Germany before independence, with Yeltsin visiting Germany in 1990 and again in 1991. Kohl would in turn become one of Yeltsin's major supporters in the West, both during the 1991 coup attempt and after.[16] While German–Russian relations have had their up-and-downs, there is no threat of open hostility. Instead economics has largely taken over from politics. Germany, for example, has provided far more financial assistance to the Russian Federation than all of the other major industrial states combined.[17]

Economic ties between the two states are not completely one-sided. As Yeltsin implemented more market reforms in the economy, Russian companies returned to what was East Germany to buy firms from the German privatization agency, *Treuhandanstalt*.[18] While relatively small, both sales were at least symbolically important. Politically, the Russian government expelled Honecker, who had fled to Moscow, and returned him to the German authorities, who wanted to bring him to trial.[19] The charges against Honecker, however, were later dropped because of illness and he was allowed to emigrate to Chile.

The overall improvement in relations also meant that lower level issues, largely ignored during the Cold War, could arise. The Volga Germans, who numbered about four million and were the largest minority in the USSR not to have their own republic, increasingly became a point of discussion between the two governments. These Soviet Germans, who were not even recognized as a nationality in the USSR, wanted to resettle in the Volga region from which they had been expelled by Stalin during World War II. After the dissolution of the USSR, the Russian government, recognizing that "their demands are warranted," attempted to find a solution.[20]

The German and Russian governments signed an agreement to provide German language broadcasts for the Volga Germans and other forms of assistance. As it turned out, some of them, like their East German brethren, also decided to vote with their feet and resettle themselves. 10,000 to 15,000 Volga Germans moved to the Kaliningrad *oblast*, which was also the disembarkation point for the WGF. They largely settled in the countryside around the capital, Kaliningrad, formerly Konigsberg. The German government initially established a "German–Russian House" for the Volga Germans and later opened a consulate in the *oblast*.[21]

The Volga Germans were not the only ones who came to Kaliningrad. German investors and tourists would also visit, aided by a rebuilt rail-line between Berlin and Kaliningrad.[22] Many of the tourists were visiting their birthplaces or the birthplaces of their ancestors. The businessmen were interested in the region's status as a free enterprise zone, which provides for tax incentives for foreign businesses.[23] Kaliningrad, which has a warm water port, has sought to become Russia's economic link to Europe instead of simply a military garrison.

The region itself was initially something of a non-issue between the two governments as both sides sought to downplay its past history. Germany had foresworn any further territorial changes in Europe after reunification, so their interests were largely commercial or nostalgic. Russia soon had its own problems with the Baltic states, one of which, Lithuania, bordered the *oblast*. In addition, some of the Kaliningrad residents began a campaign to restore Konigsberg as the official name of the city.[24]

The "Germanization" of the region, from two directions, exemplified how much relations had changed between the two former adversaries. East Prussia was fought over in the final stages of the war, occupied by Soviet troops, the native Germans displaced, and eventually the region was divided between Poland and the USSR. Now a German presence was openly encouraged and there was no outward sign of hostility on either side.[25] Much the same could be said for German–Russian relations.

THE FALL OF THE INNER EMPIRE

The Soviet withdrawal from Eastern Europe also aided the process of the dissolution of the USSR. The well-publicized sight of Soviet tanks being loaded onto railway flatcars in Hungary and Czechoslovakia could only have emboldened the nationalist forces that had been unleashed by *glasnost*. Just as some Poles had done, the Balts, Ukrainians, and others could now call for "tanks to the Volga."

Gorbachev almost certainly did not intend for the union to collapse when he started the reforms, but as in Eastern Europe, events overtook intentions. Long silent protests, especially those concerning territorial disputes, were legitimated by his policies. Some of the republican authorities began to realize that they might be better off on their own, economically, politically, and socially, even before the more radical reforms were introduced. Above all else, many people began to remember, or at least openly talk about, history.

Once Gorbachev brought up the past, the centralized Soviet state was probably doomed.[26] Since there was no longer an official version of history, long-suppressed debates and ideas re-emerged. Estonians, for example, could think back to the pre-World War II days when their standard of living was better than Finland's, instead of having a per capita income merely one-sixth of their northern neighbor. When Gorbachev acknowledged that the CPSU did not have a monopoly on the truth, the party lost its claim to rule, leading to a rapid disintegration of one half of the Soviet party-state.

The collapse of the USSR was not entirely accidental, however. As noted, Yeltsin intentionally tried to weaken the power of the central Soviet bureaucracies by building up Russia. Leaders of the independence movements in the other republics were more interested in simply breaking away from Moscow, but the effect was still the same. To a very large degree, the dissolution of Soviet authority in Eastern Europe and in the USSR mirrored each other. Yeltsin's nation-building, for example, bears a marked similarity to the efforts of East German *bezirke* authorities to weaken Honecker's centralized state apparatus.

Fundamentally, it came down to a question of ideology. Just as the East German hard-liners had feared, once communism, or more accurately state socialism, adopted market and political reforms, there was little point to it. The future of reform communism largely amounted to the introduction of western-style practices with lower living conditions. In addition, the introduction of western reforms in the WTO states meant that there was little reason or use in relying on the old instruments of control. As Gorbachev moved the USSR more in line with the West ideologically, the Soviet empire receded eastward.

The Soviets definitely did not plan for the dissolution of either the Outer or Inner Empires. The withdrawals of the Groups of Forces were very much ad hoc affairs. The Southern and Central groups had an easier time of it largely because they were smaller and in countries that were contiguous to the USSR. The WGF, on the other hand, not only had to cope with the loss of Soviet hegemony in Eastern Europe, but once they were back in the USSR, they were caught up in the fragmentation of the union and the army. The leadership had made "a grand decision as quickly as possible" and the soldiers were the ones "paying for it."[27]

For a time after the coup, the army was referred to as "the 16th republic" because it was one of the few Soviet institutions to survive. But as more and more of the republics declared their independence and began to establish their own armies, the Soviet military went the way of the union. It left an uneven legacy. To begin with, many Russian units found themselves outside Russia and frequently in the middle of an ethnic conflict. The recently-formulated Russian military doctrine allows for a permanent foreign presence in what the Russians term "the near abroad," or the other former Soviet republics. However, this is not so completely different from the defense arrangements both the British and the French made with many of their former colonies.

On the other hand, Belarus and Ukraine suddenly found themselves with large, front-line military forces due to the previous Soviet withdrawals. At one point, Belarus had twice as many tanks as Great Britain.[28] The Ukrainian Republic, with a long history of mistrust of Russia, inherited approximately 700,000 soldiers with more tanks and aircraft than any other European state aside from Russia.[29] Both states, and the Central Asian state of Kazakhstan, also had strategic nuclear weapons based on their territories. Belarus has largely cooperated with the Russian Army on military matters, but Ukraine was another matter. The Ukrainians began to seek operational control over the nuclear forces as a means of assurance against Russia, while trying to get diplomatic assurances and financial assistance from the United States.[30]

The former Soviet nuclear arsenal was, however, technically governed by the Strategic Arms Reduction Treaties signed by the United States and the USSR or its successors. The remaining Soviet conventional forces were similarly governed by the CFE Treaty, which placed limits on how much of these new arsenals Belarus and Ukraine, and Russia for that matter, could keep. Even so, the Ukrainian army, which will likely total 300,000 to 450,000 men, which would be the second largest force in Eastern Europe after Russia. Perhaps not coincidentally, Germany has also moved to reestablish its historical ties with Ukraine.

Another problem related to the withdrawals has been Russian relations with the former Baltic republics of Estonia, Latvia, and Lithuania. Gorbachev recognized their independence shortly after the attempted coup, but Soviet troops remained as part of the new Northwestern Group of Forces. While Russian authorities eventually agreed to withdraw these forces, concerns over the treatment of ethnic Russians in Estonia and Latvia led to tensions between the governments and frequent delays in these latest troop movements.

The biggest potential problem of the region, however, is the future of the Kaliningrad *oblast*, which borders Lithuania. The former Baltic republics, along with Sweden, would prefer that the Russians demilitarize the *oblast*, and, while Russia would like to cut its losses, it has not signaled a willingness to negotiate this issue. Ultimately, it seems Germany will likely replace Russia as the dominant power in the area.[31] If that comes to pass, the Russian forces in Kaliningrad will have to carry out one more withdrawal.

A NEW BEGINNING

The end of the Cold War presented those involved with new opportunities. The threat of a major conventional war in Europe, however remote it had been, was now virtually nonexistent, as was the USSR. In its place, the major countries have tried to establish a new order in Europe, and the rest of the world as well, with marginal success. The *pax Sovietica*, the post-World War II territorial status quo in Eastern Europe that was enforced by the USSR, has given way to numerous claims, disputes, and even outright war.

Even though it was outside the Soviet alliance system, no state better exemplifies this trend than the former Yugoslavia. As the federal government began to fall apart, in a near parallel to the collapse of Soviet authority, many of the Yugoslav republics moved towards independence. Slovenia, largely ethnically homogenous, achieved their independence relatively easily. In Croatia and Bosnia-Hercegovina, however, fighting broke out as ethnic Serbs in both states struggled against the new governments.

Although international efforts to resolve these two conflicts have been largely ineffective, these efforts also marked the participation of Russia as a partner with NATO to try to deal with them. Russian troops, for the first time, were part of an UN peacekeeping force, UNPROFOR (United Nations Protection Forces), which was deployed in Croatia and later expanded to Bosnia. Russia joined Britain, France, Germany, and the United States in what was called the "contact group" to seek a solution to the Bosnian crisis. No matter what the outcome of these conflicts, however, none of them entail the threat of escalation that the Cold War did.

The German government also participated in NATO efforts in the former Yugoslavia. German air force personnel flew with the NATO airborne radar planes helping to enforce the UN-mandated no-fly zones in Bosnia, the constitutionality of which nearly led to a vote of no-confidence in the Kohl government. Despite such questions about Germany's role in Europe and the problems related to unification, Germany has the chance to move forward from its former status as the divided *frontlich Stadt* (front-line state) of the Cold War. Appropriately enough, part of the former East German border fence was reconstructed, but only as a memorial.[32]

Above all else, however, it is the Russians who have another chance. If Yeltsin and the other reformers succeed in their plans for implementing western-style liberal reforms, the Russian Federation may get back to the point where it had the fastest growing economy in the world. Just as Sweden and the Netherlands adapted to their new status after giving up their hegemony by turning their attention to commerce, the Russians may yet enjoy their "Hollandization," or the loss of their empire. Whatever the ultimate results of these reforms, the Soviet withdrawal from Europe meant that "a new start has been made."[33]

Appendix 1: Commanders-in-Chief of the GSFG/WGF*

Marshal Georgy Zhukov, 1945–46. USSR Minister of Defense 1955–7.

Marshal Vassily Sokolovsky, 1946–9. Chief of the General Staff, 1952–61.

Army General Vassily Chuykov, 1949–53. Commander-in-Chief of the Ground Forces, 1960–4.

Marshal Andrey Grechko, 1953–7. USSR Minister of Defense, 1967–76.

Marshal Matvey Zakharov, 1957–60. Chief of the General Staff, 1960–63 and 1964–71.

Army General I.I. Yakubovsky, 1960–61 and 1962–65. Commander-in-Chief of the WTO, 1967–76.

Marshal Ivan Konyev, 1961–2. Commander-in-Chief of the WTO, 1955–60.

Marshal P.K. Koshevoy, 1965–9.

Army General Viktor Kulikov, 1969–71. Commander-in-Chief of the WTO, 1976–89.

Army General S.K. Kurkotkin, 1971–2.

Army General Yevgeny Ivanovsky, 1972–80.

Army General Mikhail Zaitsev, 1980–5.

Army General Pyotr Lushev, 1985–6. Commander-in-Chief of the WTO, 1989–91.

Army General Valery Belikov, 1986–7.

Army General Boris Snetkov, 1987–91.

Army General Matvey Burlakov, 1991–4.

Sources: Foreign Broadcast Information Services, *Daily Reports*; Scott and Scott, op. cit., 222; Suvorov, op. cit., 38.

Appendix 2: Chronology of Key Events[*]

1945

May 9.   Germany's unconditional surrender to Soviet forces.

June 5.   The Allied Declaration on Berlin, marking the assumption of supreme authority over Germany, comes into effect. Four occupation zones are established.

1946

April 21–22.   The SED is formed through the merger of the SPD and German communists in the Soviet zone.

1949

January 25.   CEMA is created.

April 4.   NATO is established.

May 25.   The Basic Law enters into effect, creating the FRG.

October 7.   The Constitution of the GDR enters into force.

1950

February 2.   The MfS is established in the GDR.

July 20–24.   Ulbricht is selected as First Secretary at the third SED Party Conference.

September 29.   The GDR is admitted to CEMA.

1952

May 26.   The GDR establishes a five kilometer restricted area along the inner-German border.

1953

March 5.   Stalin dies.

June 17.   Riots in East Berlin and other cities throughout the GDR. They are put down by GSFG troops.

Source: *Von der Spaltung, 1945–1991: Eine Deutsche Chronik im Texten und Bildern* (Bonn: Presse und Informationsamt der Bundersregierung, 1992).

138

1954
March 25.   The USSR recognizes the GDR as a sovereign state.

1955
May 11–14.   The WTO is established.
September 20.   The USSR signs a "Treaty of Friendship and Mutual Assistance" with the GDR.

1956
January 27.   The GDR joins the WTO.
February 14–25.   The CPSU 20th Party Congress. Khrushchev denounces Stalin in a secret speech.
October 23–November 11.   Popular uprising in Hungary, which is put down by Soviet forces.

1961
August 13–16.   The building of the Berlin Wall between East and West Berlin.

1968
April 6.   A new East German constitution is introduced.
August 21.   Soviet-led intervention in Czechoslovakia, which ended the Prague Spring.
September 26.   A *Pravda* editorial limits the sovereignty of socialist states (the Brezhnev Doctrine).

1969
September 28.   An SPD/FDP coalition wins the elections to the FRG *Bundestag*, with Brandt as chancellor.

1970
August 12.   The USSR and FRG sign a renunciation of force treaty.
December 7.   The FRG and Poland sign the Treaty of Warsaw, recognizing the Oder–Neisse line as the German–Polish border.

1971
May 3.   Ulbricht resigns as First Secretary and is succeeded by Honecker.
September 3.   Britain, France, the United States, and the USSR sign the Quadripartite Agreement on Berlin.
December 17.   The Transit Agreement between the FRG and GDR is signed in Bonn.

1972

May 26.   The SALT I agreement between the United States and the USSR is signed in Moscow.

1973

September 18.   The FRG and the GDR are simultaneously admitted to the United Nations.

July 3–12.   Opening of the CSCE.

1979

June 18.   SALT II is signed.

October 4–8.   Brezhnev announces the withdrawal of 20,000 Soviet troops and 1,000 tanks from the GDR.

December 12.   NATO decided to deploy 572 intermediate-range weapons in Western Europe beginning in 1983.

December 24.   The USSR intervenes in Afghanistan.

1980

October 17.   The INF Talks begin in Geneva.

1981

December 12.   Jaruzelski imposes martial law in Poland.

1982

June 29.   The opening of the American–Soviet Strategic Arms Reductions Talks.

October 1.   Kohl of the CDU is elected as FRG Chancellor following a constructive vote of no-confidence against Schmidt

November 10.   Brezhnev dies and is succeeded by Andropov.

1983

November 21–22.   The FRG *Bundestag* approves the deployment of the American INF launchers in West Germany.

November 24.   The USSR announces the deployment of tactical nuclear weapons in Czechoslovakia and East Germany.

1985

March 11.   Gorbachev is elected General Secretary of the CPSU following the death of Chernenko.

April 26.   The WTO is extended for twenty years.

November 19–21.   Gorbachev and Reagan meet, for the first time, in Geneva.

1986
April 26.   A fire breaks out at the Soviet nuclear power plant in Chernobyl, leading to the release of radioactive material.
October 11–12.   Gorbachev and Reagan meet in Reykjavik.

1987
January 27–28.   Gorbachev announces the policies of *glasnost* and *perestroika*.
December 12.   The INF Treaty is signed in Washington.

1988
March.   Gorbachev renounces the Brezhnev Doctrine during a state visit to Yugoslavia.

1989
February 15.   The Soviet withdrawal from Afghanistan is completed.
May 2.   Hungarian border guards remove the barbed wire fences on the Austrian–Hungarian border.
July 7.   The WTO formally revokes the Brezhnev Doctrine.
October 7.   The GDR's fortieth anniversary celebration take place, with Gorbachev in attendance.
October 18.   Honecker is relived of his duties as First Secretary of the SED and replaced by Krenz.
November 9.   The opening of the Berlin Wall.
November 13.   Modrow is elected as GDR Premier.
December 2–3.   Presidents Bush and Gorbachev meet at Malta. The Cold War is declared over.

1990
February 13.   The Ottawa Conference leads to the 2 + 4 Declaration.
March 18.   East German national elections.
May 5.   The first 2 + 4 Conference.
June 1.   Economic, monetary and social union between the FRG and the GDR.
June 22.   The second 2 + 4 Conference.
July 13–17.   The Gorbachev–Kohl summit in Moscow and the Caucasus.
July 17.   The third 2 + 4 Conference.
August 31.   The Unification Treaty is signed.

September 12.   The 2 + 4 Treaty is signed in Moscow.

October 2–3.   German unification.

October 12.   Germany and the USSR sign the Troop Presence and Withdrawal Treaty.

December 20.   Shevardnadze resigns as Foreign Minister of the USSR.

1991

June 12.   Yeltsin elected President of Russia.

June 19.   The Soviet withdrawal from Hungary is completed.

June 21.   The Soviet withdrawal from Czechoslovakia is completed.

August 19–21.   The "August Coup" attempt in the USSR.

September 6.   The Baltic republics formally secede from the USSR.

December 8.   The CIS is established by the presidents of Belarus, Russia, and Ukraine.

December 25.   Gorbachev resigns as USSR President.

1992

May 7.   The Russian Army is reestablished.

December 12.   The last Russian combat forces leave Poland.

1993

April 25.   Popular referenda in Russia. Yeltsin wins a vote of confidence.

September 8.   Russia and the United States sign a military cooperation agreement.

September 21.   Yeltsin declares emergency rule and suspends the Congress of People's Deputies.

October 3/4.   The "October Events" in Moscow.

1994

June 22.   Russia agrees to join the NATO Partnership for Peace program.

June 24.   Russia signs a trade pact with the European Union.

August 29.   Burlakov appointed as a deputy defense minister by Yeltsin.

August 31.   The formal withdrawal of the WGF from Germany.

September 6–7.   Joint American–Russian exercises in Totsk, Russia.

September 8.   Britain, France and the United States withdraw their forces from Berlin.

Appendix 3: Treaty on the Final Settlement on Germany

The Federal Republic of Germany, the German Democratic Republic, the Republic of France, the Union of Soviet Socialist Republics, the United Kingdom of Great Britain and Northern Ireland, and the United States of America –
IN THE CONSCIOUSNESS that their peoples have been living together in peace since 1945.
BEARING IN MIND the recent historic changes in Europe, which have made it possible to overcome the division of the continent.
TAKING INTO CONSIDERATION the rights and responsibilities of the Four Powers in relation to Berlin and Germany as a whole and the relevant agreements and decisions of the Four Powers during wartime and the postwar era.
DETERMINED, in accordance with their obligations arising from the United Nations Charter, to develop friendly relations between nations based on respect for the principle of equal rights and self-determination of the peoples and to take other appropriate measures to strengthen world peace.
BEARING IN MIND the principles of the final act of the Conference on Security and Cooperation in Europe. . .
IN RECOGNITION that these principles have created firm bases for the development of a just and lasting peace order in Europe,
DETERMINED to take account of the security interests of all parties,
CONVINCED of the necessity of finally overcoming differences and continuing to develop cooperation in Europe,

---

Source: ADN International Service in German 0755 GMT September 12, 1990, FBIS-WEU-177-U, September 12, 1990, 3–5.

143

IN AFFIRMATION of their readiness to strengthen security
particularly by means of effective measures for arms control
disarmament and confidence-building; their readiness not to regard
one another as enemies, but to work together toward a relationship
of trust and cooperation, and accordingly their readiness to
positively consider the creation of appropriate institutional precau
tions within the framework of the Conference on Security and
Cooperation in Europe,

IN RECOGNITION THAT the German people, in free exercise of
their right to self-determination, have demonstrated their desire to
establish the state unity of Germany, to serve peace in the world as
an equal and sovereign member of a united Europe,

IN THE CONVICTION that the unification of Germany as a state
with finally established borders is a significant contribution to peace
and stability in Europe,

IN RECOGNITION THAT through this and with the unification
of Germany as a democratic and peaceful state, the rights and
responsibility of the Four Powers in relation to Berlin and Germany
as a whole lose their significance,

REPRESENTED by their foreign ministers – who in accordance with
the declaration of 13 February 1990 in Ottawa, met on 5 May 1990 in
Bonn, on 22 June 1990 in Berlin, on 17 July [1990] in Paris with the
participation of the foreign minister of the Republic of Poland, and
on September 12 [1990] in Moscow – have agreed as follows:

Article 1

(1) The united Germany will comprise the territories of the German
Democratic Republic, the Federal Republic of Germany, and the
whole of Berlin. Its external borders shall be the borders of the
German Democratic Republic and the Federal Republic of
Germany and shall be final on the day on which this treaty comes
into force. The confirmation of the final nature of the borders of the
united Germany is an essential element in the peace order of Europe
(2) The united Germany and the Republic of Poland confirm the
border existing between in a treaty binding under international law
(3) The united Germany has no territorial claim of any kind against
other states, nor will it lay such claims in the future.

(4) The Governments of the Federal Republic of Germany and the German Democratic Republic will ensure that the Constitution of the united Germany will include no provisions which are not compatible with these principles. The applies accordingly to the provisions which are laid down in the preamble and in Article 23 section 2 and Article 146 of the Basic Law of the Federal Republic of Germany.

(5) The Governments of the Republic of France, the Union of Soviet Socialist Republics, the United Kingdom of Great Britain and Northern Ireland, and the United States of America formally accept the relevant obligations and declarations of the Governments of the Federal Republic of Germany and the German Democratic Republic and declare that with their implementation the final chapter of the borders of the united Germany is confirmed.

Article 2

The Governments of the Federal Republic of Germany and the German Democratic Republic reaffirm their declarations that only peace will emanate from German soil. According to the constitution of the united Germany, actions which are likely to disturb and are undertaken with the intentions of disturbing the peaceful coexistence of peoples, especially the conduct of a war of aggression, are unconstitutional and punishable. The Governments of Federal Republic of Germany and the German Democratic Republic declare that the united Germany will never use any of its weapons except in accordance with its Constitution and the UN Charter.

Article 3

(1) The Governments of the Federal Republic of Germany and the German Democratic Republic reaffirm their renunciation of the production and possession of and power to use nuclear, biological, and chemical weapons. They declare that the united Germany will also adhere to these obligations. In particular, the rights and responsibilities arising from the treaty on the nonproliferation of nuclear weapons of 1 July 1968 continue to be valid for the united Germany.

(2) The Government of the Federal Republic of Germany, in full
agreement with the Government of the German Democratic
Republic, made the following declaration on 30 August 1990 in
Vienna at the negotiations on conventional forces in Europe:

> "The Government of the Federal Republic of Germany under-
> takes to reduce the forces of the united Germany to a strength of
> 370,000 men (land, air, and naval forces) within three to four
> years. This reduction is to begin when the first CSCE treaty comes
> into force. Within the framework of this overall maximum, not
> more than 345,000 men will belong to the land and air forces,
> which, in accordance with the agreed mandate, are the sole subject
> of the negotiations on conventional forces in Europe. The Federal
> Government sees in its commitment to reduce land and air forces
> a significant German contribution to the reduction of conven-
> tional forces in Europe. It is assuming that in followup
> negotiations the other participants in negotiations will also
> contribute to the strengthening of security and stability in
> Europe, including measures to limit troop strengths."

The Government of the German Democratic Republic has expressly
supported this declaration.

(3) The Governments of the Republic of France, the Union of Soviet
Socialist Republics, the United Kingdom of Great Britain and
Northern Ireland, and the United States of America take note of
these declarations by the Governments of the Federal Republic of
Germany and the German Democratic Republic.

Article 4

(1) The Government of the Federal Republic of Germany, the
German Democratic Republic, and the Union of Soviet Socialist
Republics declare that the united Germany and the USSR will settle
in the form of a treaty the conditions and duration of the presence of
Soviet forces on the territory of the present-day German Democratic
Republic and Berlin, in addition to the arrangements for the
withdrawal of these forces, which will be completed by the end of the
year of 1994 in connection with the implementation of the
obligations of the Governments of the Federal Republic of

Germany and the German Democratic Republic, to which Paragraph 2 of Article 3 of this treaty relates.
(2) The Governments of the Republic of France, the United Kingdom of Great Britain and Northern Ireland, and the United States of America take note of this declaration.

Article 5

(1) Until the conclusion of the withdrawal of Soviet forces from the territory of the present-day German Democratic Republic and Berlin in accordance with Article 4 of this treaty, the only forces stationed on this territory as forces of the united Germany will be German units of territorial defense, which are not integrated into the alliance structures into which German forces are integrated in the rest of German sovereign territory. Regardless of the arrangement set out in Paragraph 2 of this article, forces of other states will not be stationed in this territory, nor will they carry out any other military activities there.
(2) For the duration of the presence of Soviet forces on the territory of the present-day German Democratic Republic and Berlin, at German request forces of the Republic of France, the United Kingdom of Great Britain and Northern Ireland, and the United States of America will remained stationed in Berlin on the basis of relevant treaty-based agreements between the government of the united Germany and the governments of the states involved. The total number of non-German forces stationed in Berlin and the extent of their equipment will not be greater than at the time of the signing of this treaty. New categories of weapons will not be introduced there by non-German forces. The government of the united Germany will conclude treaties with the governments of the states which have forces stationed in Berlin under equitable conditions and taking into account the relations existing with the states involved.
(3) After the conclusion of the withdrawal of Soviet forces from the territory of the present-day German Democratic Republic and Berlin, it will be permissible for German units to be stationed in this part of Germany which are integrated into military alliances in the same way as are those on the rest of German sovereign territory, yet without nuclear weapons carriers. This does not include conven-

tional weapons systems that can have other uses beside conventional ones, but that nevertheless are equipped for a conventional role in this part of Germany and are solely intended for this purpose. Foreign forces and nuclear weapons and their carriers will neither be stationed in this part of Germany nor transferred there.

Article 6

The right of the united Germany to belong to alliances with all the rights and duties arising from this is not affected by this treaty.

Article 7

(1) The Republic of France, the Union of Soviet Socialist Republics, the United Kingdom of Great Britain and Northern Ireland, and the United States of America herewith end their rights and responsibilities in relation to Berlin and to Germany as a whole. As a result, the relevant quadripartite agreements, resolutions and practices associated with these rights and responsibilities and all corresponding institutions of the Four Powers are thus dissolved.
(2) The united Germany accordingly has full sovereignty over its internal and external affairs.

Article 8

(1) This treaty requires ratification or adoption, which should be effected as soon as possible. The ratification will take place on the German side by the united Germany. Hence this treaty is valid for the united Germany.
(2) The documents of ratification or adoption will be lodged with the government of the united Germany. The latter will advise the governments of the other states party to the treaty of the lodging of each document of ratification or adoption.

Article 9

This treaty will come into force for the united Germany, the Republic of France, the Union of Soviet Socialist Republics, the United Kingdom of Great Britain and Northern Ireland, and the

United States of America on the day of the lodging of the last document of ratification or adoption by these states.

Article 10

The original of this treaty, the German, English, French, and Russian text of which is equally binding, will be lodged with the Government of the Federal Republic of Germany, which will pass on authenticated copies to the governments of the other states party to the treaty.

IN WITNESS WHEREOF the undersigned, the duly authorized representatives, have signed this treaty [Signed] Moscow, 12 September 1990
For the Federal Republic of Germany
For the German Democratic Republic
For the Republic of France
For the Union of Soviet Socialist Republics
For the United Kingdom of Great Britain and Northern Ireland
For the United States of America.

Notes and References

1 The Politics of Decline

1. The WGF consisted of 19 motor-rifle and tank divisions, an Air Army, and support units. The other Groups of Forces were the Northern Group of Forces in Poland with two divisions, the Southern Group of Forces in Hungary with four, and, after the 1968 WTO intervention, the Central Group of Forces in Czechoslovakia with five divisions.
2. The commander of the WGF had the authority to declare a state of emergency in East Germany. See Brian Moynahan, *Claws of the Bear* (Boston, MA: Houghton Mifflin, 1989), 397.
3. Jeffrey Gedmin, *The Hidden Hand* (Washington, DC: AEI Press, 1992), 102.
4. Moscow Television Service in Russian, July 16, 1990, Foreign Broadcast Information Service, *Daily Reports: Soviet Union* (hereafter FBIS–SOV) FBIS–SOV–90–137, July 17, 1990, 27–28.
5. See Yegor Ligachev, *Inside Gorbachev's Kremlin* (New York: Pantheon, 1993).
6. Statement by General Pavel Grachev, the Russian Minister of Defense, Russian Television Network in Russian, June 7, 1992, FBIS–SOV–92–110, June 8, 1992, 25.
7. Kenneth Waltz, *Theory of International Politics* (Reading, MA: Addison-Wesley, 1979), 79.
8. Ibid., 100.
9. Robert Gilpin, *War and Change in World Politics* (Cambridge, UK: Cambridge University Press, 1983), 28.
10. Ibid.
11. See Michael Doyle, *Empires* (Ithaca, NY: Cornell University Press, 1986).
12. Gilpin, op. cit., 29.
13. Ibid., 40.

14. Ibid., 41–4.
15. Ibid., 51.
16. Mark Elvin, *The Pattern of the Chinese Past* (Stanford, CA: Stanford University Press, 1973), 18.
17. Ibid., 18–19.
18. See William Thompson, *On Global War* (Columbia, SC: University of South Carolina Press, 1989).
19. Ibid., 52.
20. Ibid.
21. Gilpin, op. cit., 50–1.
22. Mancur Olson, *The Logic of Collective Action* (Cambridge, MA: Harvard University Press, 1977)
23. Gilpin, op. cit., 10.
24. Ibid., 11.
25. Ibid., 10, 50.
26. Paul Kennedy, *The Rise and Fall of the Great Powers* (New York: Vintage, 1989), 514.
27. Elvin, op. cit., 318.
28. Doyle, op. cit., 101.
29. Olson, *The Rise and Decline of Nations* (New Haven, CT: Yale University Press, 1982)
30. Samuel Huntington, "The US–Decline or Renewal?" *Foreign Affairs* 67, no. 5 (Winter 1988/89): 76–7.
31. Ibid., 88.
32. Kennedy, op. cit., xvi, 515.
33. Huntington, op. cit., 86.
34. See Robert Kaiser, "The USSR in Decline," *Foreign Affairs* 67, no. 5 (Winter 1989/90): 97–113. Both Huntington and Kennedy also discuss the declining fortunes of the USSR.
35. Huntington, op. cit., 86.
36. Speech to the Plenum of the Central Committee of the CPSU, 1987, cited in Gerhard Wettig, *Changes in Soviet Policy Towards The West* (Boulder, CO: Westview, 1991), 1.
37. Viktor Suvorov, *Inside the Soviet Army* (New York: Berkley, 1984), 13.
38. Rosemary Hollis, "From Force to Finance", unpublished Ph.D. dissertation, The George Washington University, 1988.
39. See Robert Keohane, *After Hegemony* (Princeton, NJ: Princeton University Press, 1984).

40. J. H. Elliott, *The Count-Duke of Olivares* (New Haven, CT: Yale University Press, 1986), 495; cited in Kennedy, op. cit., 40.
41. Kennedy, op. cit., 44.
42. Ibid., 54–5.
43. David Ziegler, *War, Peace, and International Politics* (Boston, MA: Little, Brown, 1987), 24. The German plan, called the von Schlieffen Plan, was based on detailed mobilization timetables, which were themselves keyed to railroad timetables. According to the plan, German reservists would report to their assigned stations, be shipped to the Western front to defeat France, then shifted east to deal with the Russians. The prewar improvements in both the French and Russian armies threatened the German designs, however.
44. Doyle, op. cit., 93–4.
45. Elvin, op. cit., 314.
46. Gilpin, op. cit., 19. Gilpin actually uses the more colorful terms, *classique* and *moderne* when discussing security and welfare, respectfully.
47. Ibid., 20.
48. Huntington, op. cit., 88–90. Huntington is referring to the United States, but such policies could be applied to any number of states.
49. Ibid., 87. The estimated breakdown of Soviet spending was approximately 18 percent of their GNP on defense, 26 on investment, and 56 on consumption. The higher figure of 25 percent for the military budget would, of course, decrease the other figures commensurately.
50. Both George Bush, the American president, and Gorbachev noted this point at the Malta Summit in December 1989. See Mikhail Gorbachev, "Press Conference Aboard the *Maxim Gorky*, December 3, 1991," *Perestroika and Soviet–American Relations* (Madison, CT: Sphinx Press, 1990), 251.
51. Zbigniew Brzezinski, "Post-Communist Nationalism," *Foreign Affairs* 68, no. 5 (Winter 1989/90): 1–25.

2 The GDR, GSFG and WTO

1. Moynahan, op. cit., 131.
2. Ibid.

3. Ibid., 134.
4. Ibid., 176. After the war, von Paulus chose to live in the GDR, for example.
5. Alexander Werth, *Russia at War, 1941–1945* (New York: Dutton, 1964), 553. After Stalingrad, Werth noted that the Soviet troops were "cheerful and strangely happy, and they kept shouting about the job they had done. Westward, westward. They were going west. How much better it felt than going east."
6. See John Erickson, *The Road to Berlin* (Boulder, CO: Westview, 1983).
7. Moynahan, 177. The communist-led "Lublin Poles" openly positioned themselves as an alternative to the "London Poles," which was composed of the government-in-exile.
8. Ibid., 192.
9. Harriet Scott and William Scott, *The Armed Forces of the USSR*, 3rd edn, revised and updated (Boulder, CO: Westview, 1984), 221.
10. Milovan Djilas, *Conversations With Stalin*, translated by Michael Petrovich (New York: Harcourt, Brace & World, 1962), 114.
11. The Polish Minister of Defense until 1956, for example, was Konstantin Rokossovsky, a Soviet Marshal of Polish descent. Rokossovsky had been arrested in the purges before the war and sentenced to death, but he was released when the Germans attacked in 1941. Stalin never removed his sentence, however. Suvorov, op. cit., 17–18.
12. Erickson, Lynn Hansen and William Schneider, *Soviet Ground Forces* (Boulder, CO: Westview, 1986), 24.
13. Robert Hutchings, *Soviet–East European Relations* (Madison, WI: University of Wisconsin Press, 1987), 16.
14. Christopher Jones, "Soviet Hegemony in Eastern Europe: The Dynamics of Political Autonomy," *World Politics* 26, no. 2 (January 1977): 216. Rokossovsky, who was still the Polish Minister of Defense at the time, warned Khrushchev that he could not count on the Polish Army to follow his orders.
15. Hutchings, op. cit., 25.
16. Ibid., 32.
17. Moynahan, op. cit., 394.

18. Jonathon Steele, *Soviet Power*, rev. edn (New York: Simon & Schuster, 1984), p. 92.
19. David Childs, *The GDR*, 2nd edn (London: Unwin Hyman, 1988), 118–19.
20. Ibid., 270–1.
21. Scott and Scott, op. cit. The Western allies also gave up their occupation rights over West Germany about the same time.
22. Childs, op cit., 272. As noted, that authority included the right to declare a state of emergency in the GDR.
23. Ibid., 276.
24. Ibid., 286–8. The Ministry of the Interior also controlled a diversionary unit, the Feliks Dzerzhinsky Regiment, that was equipped with American weapons and uniforms to pass as a West German unit.
25. ADN International Service (East Berlin) in German 1707 GMT March 29, 1984, Foreign Broadcast Information Service, *Daily Report: Eastern Europe* (hereafter FBIS-EEU), FBIS-EEU-84–003, March 30, 1984, AA1.
26. Aleksei Myagkov, *Inside the KGB* (New Rochelle, NY: Arlington House, 1976), 26; cited in Childs, op. cit., 289. At various points in time, the GDR shared this somewhat dubious appellation with Afghanistan, Bulgaria, and Outer Mongolia.
27. Hutchings, op. cit., 150.
28. Up until the 1980s, WTO joint exercises tended to be offensive oriented. See, for example, ADN International Service in German 1707 GMT March 29, 1984, FBIS-EEU-84–063, March 30, 1984, AA1.
29. ADN International Service in German 1526 GMT June 5, 1990, FBIS-EEU-90–109, June 6, 1990, 31.
30. Technically, the CGF was reconstituted, since the Soviet occupation forces in Austria from 1945–55 were known as the Central Group.
31. Hutchings, op. cit., 47.
32. Cited in Charles Kegley and Eugene Wittkopf, *World Politics*, 4th edn (New York: St. Martin's, 1993), 97.
33. See John Gaddis, *Strategies of Containment* (New York: Oxford University Press, 1982), 274–308.
34. East Berlin Television Service in German 1700 May 13, 1985, FBIS–SOV–85–097, May 20, 1985, F3. The East Germans'

nickname for the GSFG was "*die Freuden*" (the friends). See Ulrich Brandenburg, *The "Friends" Are Leaving* (Cologne: Bundesinstitut fur Ostwissenschftlich und International Studien, 1992).

35. Suvorov, op. cit., 52.

36. Ibid., 52–3. See Appendix 1 for a listing of the GSFG/WGF commanders.

37. Erickson, Hansen and Schneider, op. cit., 38–40. The title "Guards" was, aside from the Soviet airborne divisions which were created as Guards units, awarded to units that distinguished themselves in battle during World War II. In the war, Guards units got better equipment, pay, and personnel.

38. GSFG and NVA units were actually farther back from the border than NATO's forward units. On the other hand, the Soviet and East German forces were generally more concentrated around their bases, which would have reduced the time needed for a unit to assemble.

39. Suvorov, op. cit., 160–2. According to Suvorov, the more typical designations of Categories I, II, and III referred to the readiness status of the Military Districts. The Soviets actually had four categories; *razvertivannya* (full strength – 100 per cent), *polrazvertivannya* (normal peacetime strength – 70–80 per cent), *sokrushenno* (reduced strength – 20–50 per cent), and *kadrovaya* (very reduced strength – 5–10 per cent), but full strength was apparently only reached in wartime.

40. *Soviet Military Power, 1988* (Washington, DC: USGPO, 1988), 74–5.

41. Erickson, Hansen and Schneider, op. cit., 37, 42.

42. See *Soviet Military Power, 1989*, 44 (Washington, DC: USGPO, 1989). The OMG concept was apparently first introduced in the Hungarian Army and may have been the western OMG. See "Secret Troop Reduction," *Newsweek*, July 25, 1988, 5.

43. P. H. Vigor, *Soviet Blitzkrieg Theory* (New York: St. Martin's, 1983), x.

44. S. P. Ivanov, *Nachalnyi Period Voiny* (Moscow: Voyenizdat, 1974), cited in Vigor, op. cit., viii.

45. John Mearsheimer, *Conventional Deterrence* (Ithaca, NY: Cornell University Press, 1980), 36–7.

46. Vigor, op. cit., 184.
47. See Ibid., 183–205, for the Soviets' optimal deep battle scenario. For a fictionalized account, see either Ralph Peters, *Red Army* (New York: Pocket Books, 1989) or Steven Zaloga, *Red Thrust* (Novato, CA: Presidio, 1989).
48. Marc Fisher, "Soviet Bloc Had Detailed Plan to Invade W. Germany," *Washington Post*, March 16, 1993, A11. The plan was so detailed it included new street signs for the to-be-occupied FRG.
49. Vigor, op. cit., 202.
50. Walter Goldstein, "The Erosion of the Superpowers: The Military Consequences of Economic Distress," *SAIS Review* 8, no. 2 (Summer–Fall, 1988): 52.
51. Ibid.

3 The Beginnings of Disengagement

1. Zhores Medvedev, *Gorbachev* (Boston, MA: Little, Brown, 1986), 35–43. Gorbachev's roommate in college was Zdenk Mylnar, a Czech student, whose more Western outlook also apparently rubbed off on Gorbachev.
2. Frederick Braghoorn and Thomas Remington, *Politics in the USSR*, 3rd edn (Boston: Little, Brown, 1986), 470–1.
3. Ibid., 478.
4. Medvedev, op. cit., 117–18.
5. Ibid., 138–9.
6. It also engendered popular discontent, earning Gorbachev the nicknames of "Lemonade Joe" and *"Mineralnyy Sekretar"* (the mineral water secretary), a play on *Generalnyy Sekretar* (general secretary).
7. Political Report of the CPSU Central Committee, Moscow Television Service in Russian 0718 GMT February 25, 1986, FBIS–SOV–86–038, February 26, 1986, O2.
8. Ibid., O10.
9. Ibid. Gorbachev was referring to the need to move away from an over-reliance on extensive growth and the concurrent lack of development in intensive growth.
10. Speech to the Plenum of the Central Committee of the CPSU, January 1987, op. cit., 1.

11. Political Report to the CPSU Central Committee, op. cit., O9.
12. Ibid., O10.
13. One of the Bolsheviks purged by Stalin who was rehabilitated was Nikolai Bukharin, the principal supporter of the New Economic Policy. Shortly after his rehabilitation, Stephen Cohen's book, *Bukharin and the Bolshevik Revolution*, was published in the USSR.
14. Cited in Sylvia Woodby, "Introduction," in Woodby and Alfred Evans, Jr (eds), *Restructuring Soviet Ideology* (Boulder, CO: Westview, 1990), 2. The plan, known as the Shatalin Plan after one of the authors, called for a 500-day transition to a market economy through the privatization of state enterprises and currency reforms. The reforms were later weakened by the then Prime Minister, Nikolai Ryzkhov.
15. Political Report of the CPSU Central Committee, op. cit., O13.
16. Donald Kelly, "Gorbachev's 'New Political Thinking' and Soviet National Security Policy," in Woodby and Evans, op. cit., 132.
17. William Borders, "Report from 2 Sides in Afghan War: Soviet Soldiers Fan Out; Rebels in Caves," *New York Times*, January 8, 1980, A6.
18. See F. Stephen Larrabee and Allen Lynch, "Gorbachev: The Road to Reykjavik," *Foreign Policy* 65, (Winter 1986/87): 3–28.
19. Wettig, op. cit., 34.
20. Ibid., 40.
21. Ibid., 36. The Nicaraguan defense minister, for example, was Humberto Ortega, the brother of the former leader of the Sandinistas.
22. Strobe Talbott, *Deadly Gambits* (New York: Vintage, 1985), 30–1.
23. Ibid.
24. Western medical experts went to the USSR to assist in saving victims of the accident, while West German robots were used in the cleanup of the reactor.
25. Kenneth Currie, *Soviet Military Politics* (New York: Paragon House, 1992), 184.
26. *Soviet Military Power, 1989,* op. cit., 44.
27. "Address to the United Nations, December 7, 1988," in Gorbachev, op. cit., 203.

28. Ibid.
29. TASS in English 2222 GMT March 20, 1990, FBIS–SOV–90–055, March 21, 1990, 1.
30. Gorbachev, op. cit., 204.
31. Heinz Kessler, "Safeguarding Peace – Purpose and Aim of Our Military Activity,"*Neues Deutschland*, August 9, 1988, 3,4, FBIS-EEU-88–156, August 12, 1988, 7.
32. V. Borisenko, "We Are Parting From Our Friends," *Sovetskaya Rossiya*, May 20, 1989, FBIS–SOV–89–104, June 1, 1989, 5.
33. See ADN International Service in German 1226 GMT August 8, 1988, FBIS-EEU-88–154, August 10, 1988, 1.
34. J. F. Brown, *Surge to Freedom* (Durham, NC: Duke University Press, 1991), 50.
35. The full name of the program was the Comprehensive Program for Scientific and Technological Progress for CEMA Member Countries up to the Year 2000.
36. Brown, op. cit., 52–3.
37. Ibid., 53.
38. Gorbachev, *For a "Common European Home," For a New Way of Thinking* (Moscow: Novosti Press Agency, 1987), 16.
39. Ibid., 28.
40. TASS in English 0945 GMT December 27, 1989, FBIS–SOV–89–247, December 27, 1989, 20
41. Brown, op. cit., 61.
42. Ibid., 62.
43. Ibid., 55, 63.
44. Laszlo Bruszt and David Stark, "Remaking the Political Field in Hungary: From the Politics of Confrontation to the Politics of Competition," in Ivo Banac (ed.), *Eastern Europe in Revolution* (Ithaca, NY: Cornell University Press, 1992), 35.

4 The East German Revolution

1. See George Schopflin, Rudolf Tokes, and Ivan Volgyes, "Leadership Change and Crisis in Hungary," *Problems of Communism* 37 (September–October, 1988): 23–46.
2. Bruzst and Stark, in Banac, op. cit., 30.
3. Ibid.

4. Gedmin, op. cit., 93.
5. Banac, "Introduction," in Banac, op. cit., 2.
6. The Red Line was thought to consist of having communists as the defense and interior ministers. See Brown, op. cit., 94.
7. Ibid., 3.
8. Cited in Ibid.
9. Ibid.
10. TASS International Service in Russian 0630 GMT June 1, 1989, FBIS-SOV-89-104, June 1, 1989, 4.
11. Ibid.
12. Ibid. It was not mentioned which country or countries these observers were from, however.
13. Borisenko, op. cit., 4.
14. Ibid.
15. Ibid.
16. Ibid.
17. Ibid., 6.
18. Ivan Szelenyi, "Social and Political Landscape, Central Europe, Fall 1990," in Banac, op. cit., 226.
19. Bruzst and Stark, in Banac, op. cit., 16.
20. Norman Naimark, "'Ich will hier raus': Emigration and the Collapse of the German Democratic Republic," in Banac, op. cit., 77. It has been estimated that over an additional 17,000 East Germans had unsuccessfully attempted to flee.
21. Ibid., 73.
22. "Relations of Unprecedented Intensity and Diversity," *Neues Deutschland*, June 30, 1989, 3–4; FBIS-EEU-89-129, July 7, 1989, 39.
23. Ibid.
24. Cited in Naimark, op. cit., 81. The Soviet response was that "we are rebuilding the whole house."
25. Ibid.
26. Ibid., 83. The Hungarians would eventually let 5,000 East Germans go, despite an 1956 agreement with the GDR to return East German citizens. The Hungarian action, which had Soviet approval, angered the East German government and exacerbated GDR–Hungarian relations.
27. Gedmin, op. cit., 96.

28. Frank Sieren and Ludwig Koehne (eds), *Das Politburo* (Hamburg: Rohwohlt Taschenbuch Verlag, 1990) 97, translated and cited in Ibid., 99.
29. Ibid., 98.
30. AFP (Paris) in English 1438 GMT October 6, 1989, FBIS–SOV–89–194, October 10, 1989, 26.
31. David Keithly, *The Collapse of East German Communism* (Westport, CT: Praeger, 1992) 153. During his visit, East Germans would, ironically enough, call out *"Gorby hilft uns!"* ("help us") in addition to their demands that East Germany reform.
32. Gedmin, op. cit., 99.
33. "W.S." report, "What Do the Reformers of the SED Want? A Report on the Situation From the Leadership of the Party," *Welt am Sontag,* October 8, 1989, 2, FBIS-EEU-89–195, October 11, 1989, 22.
34. "Gorbatschow kritisert Honecker: Stasi nauppelt Verzwerfelte nieder," *Die Welt,* October 9, 1989, 1, translated and cited in Gedmin, op. cit., 99.
35. Craig Whitney, "Soviet Forces Were Ordered to Stay in Barracks, East Germans Say," *Washington Post,* December 3, 1989, A1.
36. Gedmin, op. cit., 63–4.
37. Ibid.
38. Ibid., 101.
39. Brown, op. cit., 146.
40. Rupert Scholz and Manfred Schell, "GDR Minister for Disarmament Rainer Eppelman in Discussion with Former Minister of Defence Scholz: 'The Politicians Told the Border Soldier: Just Pull the Trigger and Cut Him Down,'" *Die Welt,* July 10, 1990, 6, Foreign Broadcast Information Services, *Daily Report: Western Europe* (hereafter FBIS-WEU) FBIS-WEU-90–155–U, August 10, 1990, 22.
41. Gedmin, op. cit., 101–2.
42. Ibid., 102.
43. The deputy commander-in-chief of the Joint Forces of the Warsaw Pact in the NVA, who was always a Soviet officer, attended all high level NVA meetings, for example.

44. Keithly, op. cit., 160.
45. Ibid., 161.
46. Gedmin, op. cit., 103.
47. Ibid., 105.
48. Bruszt and Stark, op. cit., 17.
49. Egon Krenz, *Wenn Mauren Fallen* (Vienna: Paul Neff Verlag, 1990), 25, translated and cited in Gedmin, op. cit., 106.
50. Moscow Television Service in Russian 1530 GMT September 26, 1989, FBIS–SOV–89–187, September 28, 1989, 29–30.
51. Gedmin, op. cit., 107.
52. Ibid., 108.
53. Vladimir Markov, "Two Systems, One Nation," *Frankfurter Rundschau*, November 17, 1989, 2, FBIS–SOV–89–222, November 20, 1989, 33.
54. Ibid.
55. Ibid.
56. Ibid., 109.
57. Scholz and Schell, op. cit., 22–3.
58. Ibid., 110.
59. Ibid., 111. Supposedly, Markus Wolf, the former head of the MfS's foreign intelligence operations and a major East German supporter of *perestroika*, was also present at these meetings.
60. M. Podklyuchnikov, "GDR: Government Program Approved," *Pravda*, November 19, 1989, 5, FBIS–SOV–89–223, November 21, 1989, 20. The new government included members of the SED, the Liberal Democratic Party, the East German CDU, the National Democratic Party, and the Democratic Peasants' Party.
61. V. Lapsky, "Policy Statement," *Izvestiya*, November 20, 1989, 3, FBIS–SOV–89–223, 19.
62. "Guarantees of Stability; World Press on Events in GDR," *Sovetskaya Rossiya*, November 15, 1989, 5, FBIS–SOV–89–223, 27. The leader of the New Democracy movement had stated the GDR would remain socialist but "it will be a new, democratic type of socialism."
63. Lapsky, op. cit., 20.
64. Ibid.
65. TASS in English 2324 GMT November 20, 1989, FBIS–SOV–223, 27.

66. S. Baygarov, S. Zyubanov, and M. Podklyuchnikov, "At SED Extraordinary Congress," *Pravda*, December 17, 1989, 8, FBIS–SOV–89–242, December 19, 1989, 23.
67. S. Baygarov, S. Zyubanov, and M. Podklyuchnikov, "Extraordinary Congress Over," *Pravda*, December 18, 1989, 8, FBIS–SOV–89–242, 24.
68. Moscow Television Service in Russian 1500 GMT December 17, 1989, FBIS–SOV–89–241, December 18, 1989, 32.
69. Ibid.
70. Lapsky, "GDR: Difficult Path to Stabilization," *Izvestiya*, November 21, 1989, 4, FBIS–SOV–89–223, 25.
71. Ibid.
72. TASS in English 2202 GMT November 20, 1989, FBIS–SOV–89–223, p. 26.
73. TASS in English 1736 GMT December 18, 1989, FBIS–SOV–89–242, p. 23.
74. "How Should Germany Be United," *Pravda*, February 2, 1990, 4, FBIS–SOV–90–123, February 2, 1990, 31.
75. Iris Lush, "There Must Be No Delay. Thoughts on the Origins of Neofascism in the GDR," *Krasnaya Zvezda*, January 31, 1990, 3, FBIS–SOV–90–123, 33.
76. Joachim Neander, *Die Welt*, March 16, 1990, 5, FBIS-WEU-90–052, March 16, 1990, 6.
77. Podklyuchnikov, "The Party is Starting With Itself," *Pravda*, January 25, 1990, 6, FBIS–SOV–90–026, February 7, 1990, 28.
78. *Bild*, March 16, 1990, 1, 4, FBIS-WEU-90–052, 10.
79. Ibid.
80. Ibid.
81. Ibid. There were also reports that the KGB assumed control of "whole contingents of former employees" of the MfS, which were discounted "as absolute nonsense" by Wolf. See ADN International Service in German 1900 GMT June 11, 1990, FBIS-EEU-90–113, June 12, 1990, 30.
82. Markov, op. cit.
83. Ibid.
84. Ibid.
85. DPA (Hamburg) in German 1055 GMT December 16, 1989, FBIS-WEU-89–246, December 26, 1989, 5.

86. ADN International Service in German 2146 GMT November 29, 1989, FBIS–SOV–89–229, November 30, 1989, 1.
87. Ibid.
88. Ibid.
89. TASS International Service in Russian 1655 GMT December 18, 1989, FBIS–SOV–89–242, 20.
90. TASS in English 1302 GMT February 2, 1990, FBIS–SOV–90–123, 33.
91. TASS International Service in Russian 1655 GMT December 18, 1989. This practice was known in the USSR as *subbotnik*, which was one day a month, typically a Saturday, when workers would provide a free day of labor to the state.
92. "Instead of Aid–Espionage?" *Pravda*, December 27, 1989, 5, FBIS–SOV–89–248, December 28, 1989, 25.
93. Ibid.
94. Ibid.
95. "Cooperation of Equals," *Rabochaya Tribuna*, January 25, 1990, 3, FBIS–SOV–90–123, 30.
96. Moscow International Service in Mandarin 1400 GMT December 16, 1989 FBIS–SOV–89–241, December 18, 1989, 3.
97. Ibid.

5 The WGF and Moscow's Relations with Germany

1. Brown, op. cit., 58.
2. Ibid.
3. Boris Averchenko and Leonid Zhymrev, "True Socialism Is Our Choice," *Pravda*, December 4, 1989, 5, FBIS–SOV–89–231, December 4, 1989, 55.
4. Moscow Domestic Service in Russian 1645 GMT April 21, 1990, FBIS–SOV–90–078, April 23, 1990, 7.
5. Ibid.
6. Moscow International Service in Polish 1500 GMT February 11, 1990, FBIS–SOV–90–030, February 13, 1990, 29.
7. "In a Friendly Atmosphere," *Pravda*, March 22, 1990, 5, FBIS–SOV–90–057, March 23, 1990, 19.
8. PAP (Warsaw) in English 1702 GMT April 13, 1990, FBIS–SOV–90–074, April 17, 1990, 3.

9. A. Borovkov, "Homeward Bound," *Krasnaya Zvezda*, March 21, 1990, 3, FBIS–SOV–90–057, 19.
10. TASS in English 1901 GMT February 6, 1990, FBIS–SOV–90–026, February 7, 1990, 30. Like the Poles, the Czechs shouted for the "Occupiers, out" and "Russians, out."
11. Moscow Television Service in Russian 1530 GMT September 26, 1989, op. cit.
12. Naimark, op. cit., 94.
13. Ye. Bovkun, "The German Question: Outlines and Reality," *Izvestiya*, November 27, 1989, 3, FBIS–SOV–89–231, 54.
14. Ibid.
15. Ibid.
16. "Europarliament on Chancellor Kohl's Plans–TASS Comments," TASS in English 1823 GMT December 15, 1989, FBIS–SOV–89–241, 31.
17. Moscow Domestic Service in Russian 1230 GMT, December 10, 1989, FBIS–SOV–89–237, December 12, 1989, 6.
18. Ibid.
19. See Strobe Talbot and Michael Beschloss, *At the Highest Levels* (Boston, MA: Little, Brown, 1993).
20. Naimark, op. cit.
21. DPA in German 1017 GMT December 11, 1989, FBIS-WEU-89–246, December 11, 1989, 10. The Western ambassadors were Vernon Walters for the United States, Sir Christopher Mallaby for the United Kingdom, and Serge Boidevaix for France.
22. Ibid., 11.
23. Moscow World Service in English 1210 GMT February 21, 1990, FBIS–SOV–90–039, February 27, 1990, 7.
24. Warsaw Domestic Service in Polish 1530 GMT February 21, 1990, FBIS-EEU-90–036, February 22, 1990, 64.
25. Moscow Domestic Service In Russian 1600 GMT March 1, 1990, FBIS–SOV–90–043, March 5, 1990, 9.
26. ADN International Service in German 1559 GMT June 5, 1990, FBIS-EEU-90–109, June 6, 1990, 31.
27. ADN International Service in German 1931 GMT June 5, 1990, FBIS-EEU-90–109.
28. Vladimir Ostrovsky, "We Cannot Agree to an Imbalance of Forces," *Zolnierz Wolnosci*, March 20, 1990, 7, FBIS–SOV–90–057, March 23, 1990, 17.

29. Rolf Gunther, "Balance of Security–Core of the German Question," *Neues Deutschland*, February 9, 1990, 6, FBIS–SOV–90–131, February 14, 1990, 26.
30. Ibid.
31. Ulrich Deupmann, "Moscow Makes NATO Transformation Into Political Alliance Condition for Germany's Membership," *Suddeutsche Zeitung*, June 11, 1990, FBIS-EEU-90–113, June 12, 1990, 27.
32. Kull, op. cit., 142.
33. Montreal International Service in English 1930 GMT, February 16, 1990, FBIS–SOV–90–034, February 20, 1990, 11.
34. Deupmann, op. cit.
35. Ibid.
36. Aleksandr Antsiferov, "Helmut Kohl's Visit," TASS in English 2107 GMT July 13, 1990, FBIS–SOV–90–138, July 10, 1990, 9.
37. Ibid.
38. "Encounter at Stavrapallo," *The Economist*, July 21, 1990, 47.
39. ADN International Service in German 1447 GMT August 2, 1990, FBIS-WEU-90–150–U, August 3, 1990, 8.
40. Ibid.
41. Ibid.
42. "Encounter at Stavrapallo," op. cit.
43. Ibid.
44. Ibid.
45. Ibid. The reference is to the 1922 Treaty of Rapallo between the German Weimar Republic and Soviet Russia, which established diplomatic relations between the two countries.
46. "The New Math in Moscow," *Newsweek*, September 24, 1990, 36.
47. Ibid., 48. The Oder and Neisse rivers became the border between Poland and Germany after World War II, when Poland acquired the regions of Pomerania and Silesia.
48. DPA in German 1155 GMT August 31, 1990, FBIS-WEU-90–170–U, August 31, 1990, 4.
49. ADN International Service in German 1832 GMT August 29, 1990, FBIS-WEU-90–169–U, August 30, 1990, 1.
50. DPA in German 1027 GMT August 31, 1990, FBIS-WEU-90–170–U.

51. DPA in German 1614 GMT September 7, 1990, FBIS-WEU-90–175–U, September 10, 1990, 1.
52. ADN International Service in German 1319 GMT September 3, 1990, FBIS-WEU-90–171–U, September 4, 1990, 1.
53. "Rispe" report, "Ammunition for Multiple Rocket Launchers Withdrawn," *Der Morgen*, July 25, 1990, 2, FBIS-WEU-90–146–U, July 30, 1990, 5.
54. NZ/ADN report, "Military Training Abroad Stopped," *Neue Zeit*, August 31, 1990, 4, FBIS-WEU-90–171–U, 7.
55. ADN International Service in German 0931 GMT June 6, 1990, FBIS-EEU-90–109, June 6, 1990, 30.
56. ADN International Service in German September 11, 1990, FBIS-WEU-90–176–U, September 11, 1990, 4.
57. ADN International Service in German 1711 GMT September 10, 1990, FBIS-WEU-90–176–U, 3.
58. ADN International Service in German 1759 GMT September 11, 1990, FBIS-WEU-90–177–U, September 12, 1990, 2.
59. DPA in German 0718 GMT September 12, 1990, FBIS-WEU-90–177–U, 3. See Appendix 3 for the complete text of the treaty.
60. DPA in German 0719 GMT September 13, 1990, FBIS-WEU-90–178–U, September 13, 1990, 7.
61. Ibid.
62. DPA in German 1022 GMT September 24, 1990, FBIS-WEU-90–185–U, September 24, 1990, 1.
63. Ibid.
64. TASS in English 0850 GMT October 3, 1990, FBIS-WEU-90–192–U, October 3, 1990, 25.
65. Rudiger Moniac, "Creating Unity of the Army With Great Care," *Die Welt*, October 2, 1990, 6, FBIS-WEU-90–192–U, 24.
66. Moniac, "Stoltenberg's Planning Chief Commander in the GDR," *Die Welt*, August 27, 1990, 1, FBIS-WEU-90–168–U, August 29, 1990, 2.
67. Ibid.
68. Ibid.
69. ADN International Service in German 1747 GMT October 24, 1990, FBIS-WEU-90–208, October 26, 1990, 9.
70. ADN International Service in German 1543 GMT October 25, 1990, FBIS-WEU-90–208, 9.

71. Ibid.
72. *Frankfurter Allgemeine*, May 22, 1991, 2, FBIS-WEU-91-100, May 23, 1991, 6.
73. TASS International Service in Russian 1748 September 18, 1990, FBIS-WEU-90-182-U, September 19, 1990, 1.
74. I. Kosenko, "T. Hoffman: We Did Our Duty Honorably," *Krasnaya Zvezda*, October 2, 1990, 3, FBIS-WEU-90-192-U, 24.
75. "MG" report, "Basic Principles of Merger," *Welt am Sontag*, September 16, 1990, 7, FBIS-WEU-90-182-U, 3.
76. Ivanka Khelbarova, "'Superfluous' Arsenal Tease the Appetites of Former Alliance Members," *Duma*, February 11, 1991, 4, FBIS-EEU-91-032, February 11, 1991, 2.
77. "MG" report, op. cit.
78. Ibid.
79. "Elements of a New Strategy," *Pravda*, July 23, 1990, 4, FBIS–SOV-90-144, July 26, 1990, 3.
80. An Agreement on Transitory Measures had already been signed on October 9. See Brandenburg, op. cit., 9–10.
81. ADN International Service in German 1543 GMT October 25, 1990.
82. Lothar Ruhl, "Does Bonn Have to Pay for the Soviet Army?" *Die Welt*, April 7–8, 1990, 1, FBIS-WEU-90-069, April 10, 1990, 10.
83. Nikolay Burbyga and Sergey Mostovshchikov, "Matvey Burlakov, Commander of the Western Group of Forces: We Are Not Trading in Weapons," *Izvestiya*, March 30, 1992, 2, FBIS–SOV-92-065, April 3, 1992, 11.
84. Ibid.
85. Ibid.
86. DPA in German 1238 GMT July 10, 1991, FBIS-WEU-91-113, July 11, 1991, 5.
87. Bill Gwertz, "Yazov Trip Strains German–Soviet Ties," *Washington Times*, April 4, 1991, A8.
88. Burbyga and Mostovshchikov, op. cit.
89. "Fwm/Dit," "GDR: 100 Russians Deserted – Order to Shoot in Barracks," *Bild am Sontag*, September 23, 1990, 2, FBIS-WEU-90-187, September 26, 1990, 3.

90. TASS International Service in Russian 1740 GMT July 4, 1991, FBIS–SOV–91–129, July 5, 1991, 31. The WGF procuracy conducted a joint investigation of the incident with the Leipzig police and prosecutor's office.
91. Lapsky, "Service Takes Its Course," *Izvestiya*, February 8, 1990, 4, FBIS–SOV–90–030, February 13, 1990, 28.
92. ADN International Service in German 0849 GMT September 12, 1990, FBIS-WEU-90–177–U, 7.
93. "Fwm/Dit," op. cit.
94. Burbyga and Mostovshchikov, op. cit.
95. ADN International Service in German 1302 GMT October 2, 1990, FBIS-WEU-90–192–U, 30.
96. ADN International Service in German 1135 GMT September 12, 1990, FBIS-WEU-90–178–U, 3.
97. Moynahan, op. cit., 169.

6 Domestic Politics and the WGF

1. Jacques Amalria and Sylvia Kauffman, *Le Monde*, March 9, 1990, FBIS-EEU-90–47, March 9, 1990, 64.
2. Bratislava Domestic Service in Slovak 1630 GMT August 2, 1990, FBIS-EEU-90–150, August 3, 1990, 10.
3. Budapest Domestic Service in Hungarian 0600 GMT July 14, 1990, FBIS-EEU-90–136, July 16, 1990, 27.
4. CTK (Prague) in English 2000 GMT January 16 1991, FBIS-EEU-91–014, January 17, 1991, 19.
5. MTI (Budapest) in English 1026 GMT May 12, 1992, FBIS-EEU-92–095, May 15, 1992, 19.
6. Michael Meyer, "Pullout of the 'Barbarians,'" *Newsweek*, June 10, 1991, 36.
7. See Radek Sikorski, "The Red Army Remains," *The National Review*, February 25, 1991, 22.
8. CTK in English 1120 GMT June 22, 1991, FBIS–SOV–91–121, June 24, 1991, 24; Interfax in English 1500 GMT June 20, 1991, FBIS–SOV–91–121, 25.
9. MTI in English 1554 GMT June 10, 1991, FBIS-EEU-91–112, June 11, 1991, 27; CTK in English 1342 GMT June 25, 1991, FBIS-EEU-91–123, June 26, 1991, 9.

10. "New Chief of USSR Troops in Germany," *Neues Deutschland*, December 13, 1990, 3, FBIS-WEU-90–242, December 17, 1990, 14.
11. Warsaw Domestic Service in Polish 1530 GMT February 21, 1990, FBIS-EEU-90–036, February 22, 1990, 64.
12. PAP in English 1609 GMT January 21, 1992, FBIS-EEU-92–014, January 22, 1992, 20. Russian President Yeltsin would later speed up the withdrawal as a show of support for the Polish government.
13. Michael Albrecht, "Departure for New Shores?" *Neue Zeit*, June 6, 1990, 2, FBIS-EEU-90–113, June 12, 1990, 26.
14. Ibid.
15. David White, "The Empire Splits Up," *The Financial Times*, December 22, 1992, 10.
16. Alvin Rubinstein, *Soviet Foreign Policy Since World War II*, 4th edn (New York: HarperCollins, 1992), 120.
17. Ligachev, op. cit.
18. Rubinstein, op. cit., 118.
19. Moscow Domestic Service in Russian 1645 GMT April 21, 1990, FBIS–SOV–90–078, April 23, 1990, 7.
20. "Federal Property Office in Cottbus Registers Soviet Facilities," *Die Morgen*, May 15, 1991, 17, FBIS-WEU-91–100, May 23, 1991, 6.
21. Ibid.
22. Interfax (Moscow) in English 1311 July 8, 1992, FBIS–SOV–92–133, July 10, 1992, 29.
23. Burbyga and Mostovshchikov, op. cit.
24. D.G./hrh report, "Schwerin: Soviet Withdrawal Slower Than Expected," *Die Welt*, February 13, 1991, 8, FBIS-WEU-91–034, February 20, 1991, 13.
25. Ibid.
26. Ibid.
27. ADN International Service in German 1319 GMT September 3, 1990.
28. Burbyga and Mostovshchikov, op. cit.
29. Ibid.
30. Ibid.
31. DPA in German 1631 GMT March 21, 1991, FBIS-WEU-91–056, March 222, 1991, 8.

32. Ibid., 11.
33. ADN in German 1002 GMT August 5, 1991, FBIS-WEU-91–151, August 6, 1991, 13.
34. Ibid. According to Soviet tables of organization and equipment, a full-strength motor-rifle battalion had 455 men.
35. ADN in German 0923 GMT May 22, 1991, FBIS-WEU-91–100, 7.
36. Burbyga and Mostovshchikov, op. cit., 11.
37. V. Izgarshev, "We Serve the Fatherland," *Pravda*, May 7, 1990, 6, FBIS–SOV–90–090, May 9, 1990, 64.
38. A. Vasilets and I. Kosenko, "Deepening Perestroyka by Deeds, From the Western Group of Forces Party Conference," *Krasnaya Zvezda*, June 8, 1990, 2, FBIS–SOV–90–113, June 12, 1990, 73.
39. Ibid., 74.
40. S. Popov, "Activeness of Thought and Action," *Krasnaya Zvezda*, February 22, 1991, 1, FBIS–SOV–91–038, February 26, 1991, 29.
41. Michael Dobbs, "Soviet General Faces Challenge; Yaroslavl Voters Get a Choice on Sunday," *Washington Post*, March 24, 1990, A1.
42. DPA in German 1937 GMT August 26, 1991, FBIS-WEU-91–166, August 27, 1991, 6.
43. Anna Tomforde, "German Pullout 'Will Continue,'" *The Guardian*, August 20, 1991, 4.
44. "H. S." report, "Former NVA Soldiers Loyal in Crisis," *Welt am Sontag*, August 25, 1991, FBIS-WEU-91–166.
45. Ibid.
46. Meyer, "Kaliningrad: The Old Guard Hangs On," *Newsweek*, September 16, 1991, 39.
47. DPA in German 1937 GMT August 26, 1991, op. cit.
48. Fred Hiatt, "Russia Establishes a Defense Ministry," *Washington Post*, March 17, 1992, A10.
49. John Morrison, *Yeltsin: Bolshevik or Democrat?* (New York: Dutton, 1991). The Soviets intentionally left Russia weak, in part because the All-Union ministries were based in Moscow anyway and in part to prevent Russia from emerging as a possible counter.

50. Yelena Agapova, "Before You Form an Army You Should Know What It Is For, Expert Andrey Kokoshin Believes," *Krasnaya Zvezda*, March 17, 1992, 2, FBIS–SOV–92–053, March 18, 1992, 26.
51. Ibid.
52. Ibid.
53. A. Dokuchayev, "I Favor 'Ground Defense Forces,'" *Krasnaya Zvezda*, November 28, 1991, 2, FBIS–SOV–91–232, December 3, 1991, 47.
54. Mearshiemer, op. cit., 50–1.
55. Russian Television Network in Russian, June 7, 1992, op. cit.
56. PAP in English 1444 GMT January 17, 1992, FBIS-EEU-92–013, January 21, 1992, 25. In March 1992, the official name of the WGF was changed to "the Western Group of Forces of the Russian Federation." Brandenburg, op. cit., 42.
57. Brandenburg, op. cit., 42–3.
58. Ibid.
59. Yury Teplyakov, "Quiet as a Church Mouse, Heads Down Low," *Der Morgen*, May 21, 1991, 3, FBIS–SOV–91–108, June 5, 1991, 26–7.
60. Ibid., 26.
61. Ibid., 27.
62. Fred Hiatt, "GIs Finding Friends Among Former Foes," *Washington Post*, September 7, 1994, A23.
63. Interfax in English 1432 GMT May 12, 1991, FBIS–SOV–92–093, May 13, 1992, 35.
64. John Lloyd, "Corruption Charges Threaten Yeltsin's Referendum Hopes," *Financial Times*, April 23, 1993, 1.
65. Brandenburg, op. cit., 16–17.
66. CTK in English 1346 GMT June 15, 1991, FBIS-EEU-91–123, June 26, 1991, 9; F. Lukyanov, "Hungary: Solemn Farewell," *Izvestiya*, June 15, 1991, 4, FBIS–SOV–91–121, 25.
67. Russian Television Network in Russian 0831 GMT August 31, 1994, FBIS–SOV–94–169, August 31, 1994, 3. Actually the Russians did not completely leave on August 31. A special detail of the Berlin Brigade stayed behind to clean up the former WGF facilities and the Russians retained the use of the Sperenburg airbase until September 7.

7 The Withdrawal and the End of the Cold War

1. See the statement by Georgy Arbatov, the Director of the Institute for Canada and the USA, in Kegley and Wittkopf, op. cit., 109.
2. Lyudmila Alekseeva, *The Thaw Generation* (Pittsburgh, PA; University of Pittsburgh Press, 1993).
3. Angus Roxburgh, *The Second Russian Revolution* (Cambridge, UK: Cambridge University Press, 1993), 5.
4. Kennedy, op. cit., 59.
5. Ibid.
6. Peter Gladkov, a Policy Analyst at the Institute for Canada and the USA, noted that "[t]he Cold War ended because it was no longer feasible. The US and USSR had exhausted their capacity to carry on their global confrontation." Cited in Kegley and Wittkopf, op. cit.
7. Rubinstein, op. cit., 119.
8. A. Kortunov and A. Izyumov, "What To Understand By State Interests in Foreign Policy," *Literaturnaya Gazeta*, no. 28, July 11, 1990, 14, FBIS–SOV–90–138, July 18, 1990, 11.
9. Pawel Ziolek, "Europe Will Not Be Europe Without Russia," *Zycie Warszawy*, August 4–5, 1990, 1, FBIS–WEU–90–153–U, August 8, 1990, 12.
10. Nataliya Izyumova, "Foreign Policy: The Russian Dimension," *Moskovskiye Novosti*, no. 6, February 10, 1991, 12, FBIS–SOV–91–040, 67.
11. Ibid.
12. ITAR-TASS in English 1929 GMT August 18, 1992, FBIS–SOV–92–161, August 19, 1992, 12.
13. Kortunov and Izyumov, op. cit., 15.
14. Radio Moscow World Service in English 1310 GMT October 3, 1991, FBIS–SOV–91–194, October 7, 1991, 29.
15. Deutschlandfunk Network (Cologne) in German 1100 GMT September 17, 1990, FBIS–WEU–90–181, September 18, 1990, 13.
16. Quentin Peel, David Buchan, and Charles Leadbeater, "Kohl Speaks Out in Support of Yeltsin," *Financial Times*, March 16, 1993, 2.

17. Judy Dempsey and William Keeling, "Kohl Warns Russia Will Need Much More Aid," *Financial Times*, April 6, 1993, 1.
18. "Russian Investors Acquire Two Eastern German Companies," *This Week in Germany*, June 25, 1993, 4.
19. Moscow Radio Rossii Network in Russian 1300 GMT November 16, 1991, FBIS–SOV–91–222, November 18, 1991, 55.
20. Deutschlandfunk Network in German 1105 GMT November 17, 1991, FBIS–SOV–91–222, 56.
21. Quentin Peel, "Railway Renews Germany's Links to East Prussian Past," *Financial Times* May 25, 1993, 18.
22. Ibid.
23. Margaret Shapiro, "Russian City Banks Future on Past Enemy," *Washington Post*, June 8, 1993, A14.
24. Ibid.
25. Ibid.
26. See David Remnick, *Lenin's Tomb* (New York: Random House, 1993).
27. Burbyga and Mostovshchikov, op. cit., 11.
28. White, op. cit.
29. Ibid.
30. Steve Coll and R. Jeffrey Smith, "Ukraine Could Seize Control Over Nuclear Arms," *Washington Post*, June 3, 1993, A1.
31. Peel, op. cit.
32. "A Part of the Intra-German Border to Arise Anew (as a Memorial)," *This Week in Germany*, June 4, 1993, 7.
33. DPA in German 1242 GMT September 12, 1990, FBIS-WEU-90–177–U, September 12, 1990, 6.

Selected Bibliography

Articles

"A Part of the Intra-German Border to Arise Anew," *This Week in Germany*, (June 4, 1993) p. 7.

Brzezinski, Zbigniew. "Post-Communist Nationalism," *Foreign Affairs* 68, no. 5 (Winter 1989/90) pp. 1–25.

Goldstein, Walter. "The Erosion of the Superpowers: The Military Consequences of Economic Distress," *SAIS Review* 8, no. 2 (Summer–Fall, 1988) pp. 51–68.

Gwertz, Bill. "Yazov Trip Strains German–Soviet Ties," *Washington Times* (April 4, 1991) A8.

Huntington, Samuel. "The US–Decline or Renewal?" *Foreign Affairs* 67, no. 5 (Winter 1988/89) pp. 76–96.

Jones, Christopher. "Soviet Hegemony in Eastern Europe: The Dynamics of Political Autonomy," *World Politics* 26, no. 2 (Jan. 1977) pp. 216–241.

Kaiser, Robert. "The USSR in Decline," *Foreign Affairs* 67, no. 5 (Winter 1988/89) pp. 97–113.

Larrabee, F. Stephen and Allen Lynch. "Gorbachev: The Road to Reykjavik," *Foreign Policy* 65, (Winter 1986/87) pp. 3–28.

Meyer, Michael. "Pullout of the 'Barbarians,'" *Newsweek* (June 10, 1991) p. 36.

—— "Kaliningrad: The Old Guard Hangs On," *Newsweek* (Sept. 16, 1991) p. 39.

"Russian Investors Acquire Two Eastern German Companies," *This Week in Germany* (June 25, 1993) p. 4.

Schopflin, George, Rudolf Tokes, and Ivan Volgyes. "Leadership Change and Crisis in Hungary," *Problems of Communism* 37, (Sept.–Oct. 1988) pp. 23–46.

"Secret Troop Reduction," *Newsweek*, July 25, 1988 p. 5.

Sikorski, Radek. "The Red Army Remains," *The National Review* (February 25, 1991) pp. 22–4.

"The New Math In Moscow," *Newsweek* (Sept. 24, 1990) p. 36.

Books

Alekseeva, Lyudmila (1993) *The Thaw Generation: Coming of Age in the Post-Stalin Era*, Pittsburgh, PA: University of Pittsburgh Press.

Amin, Saikal and William Maley (eds) (1989) *The Soviet Withdrawal From Afghanistan*, Cambridge, UK: Cambridge University Press.

Banac, Ivo (ed.) (1992) *Eastern Europe in Revolution*, Ithaca, NY: Cornell University Press.

Barghoorn, Frederick and Thomas Remington (1986) *Politics in the USSR*, 3rd edn, Boston, MA: Little, Brown.

Barry, Donald and Carol Barner-Barry (1991) *Contemporary Soviet Politics: An Introduction*, 4th edn, Englewood Cliffs, NJ: Prentice-Hall.

Brown, J. F. (1991) *Surge to Freedom: The End of Communist Rule in Eastern Europe*, Durham, NC: Duke University Press.

Childs, David (1988) *The GDR: Moscow's German Ally*, 2nd edn, London: Unwin Hyman.

Currie, Kenneth (1992) *Soviet Military Politics: Contemporary Issues*, New York: Paragon House.

Dallin, Alexander and Condeleeza Rice (eds) (1986) *The Gorbachev Era*, Stanford, CA: Stanford Alumni Association.

Dawisha, Karen (1990) *Eastern Europe, Gorbachev, and Reform: The Great Challenge*, 2nd edn, Cambridge, UK: Cambridge University Press.

Doyle, Michael (1986) *Empires*, Ithaca, NY: Cornell University Press.

Djilas, Milovan (1962) *Conversations with Stalin*, Tr. Michael Petrovich. New York: Harcourt, Brace & World.

Elliott, J. H. (1986) *The Count-Duke of Olivares: The Statesman In an Age of Decline*, New Haven, CT: Yale University Press.

Elvin, Mark (1973) *The Pattern of the Chinese Past*, Stanford, CA: Stanford University Press.

Erickson, John (1983) *The Road to Berlin: Continuing the History of Stalin's War with Germany*, Boulder, CO: Westview.

—— Lynn Hansen and William Schneider (1986) *Soviet Ground Forces: An Operational Assessment*, Boulder, CO: Westview.

Gaddis, John (1982) *Strategies of Containment: A Critical Appraisal of Postwar American National Security Policy*, New York: Oxford University Press.

Gati, Charles (1990) *The Bloc That Failed: Soviet–East European Relations in Transition*, Bloomington, IN; Indiana University Press.

Gedmin, Jeffrey (1992) *The Hidden Hand: Gorbachev and the Collapse of East Germany*, Washington, DC: AEI Press.

Gilpin, Robert (1983) *War and Change in World Politics*, Cambridge, UK: Cambridge University Press.

Gorbachev, Mikhail (1987) *Perestroika: New Thinking for Our Country and the World*, New York: Harper and Row.

—— (1990) *Perestroika and Soviet–American Relations*, Madison, CT: Sphinx.

Hollis, Rosemary (1988) *From Force to Finance: British Adaptation to Decline: Transforming Relations with Selected Arab Gulf State*, unpublished Ph.D. dissertation, The George Washington University.

Hutchings, Robert (1987) *Soviet–East European Relations: Consolidation and Conflict*, Madison, WI: University of Wisconsin Press.

Keohane, Robert (1984) *After Hegemony*, Princeton, NJ: Princeton University Press.

Kegley, Charles and Eugene Wittkopf (1993) *World Politics: Trend and Transformation*, 4th edn, New York: St. Martin's.

Kennedy, Paul (1989) *The Rise and Fall of the Great Powers*, New York: Vintage.

Keithly, David (1992) *The Collapse of East German Communism: The Year the Wall Came Down, 1989*, Westport, CT: Praeger.

Ligachev, Yegor (1993) *Inside Gorbachev's Kremlin*, New York: Pantheon.

Luttwak, Edward (1983) *The Grand Strategy of the Soviet Union*, New York: St. Martin's.

Mastny, Vojtech (1979) *Russia's Road to the Cold War: Diplomacy, Warfare and the Politics of Communism*, New York: Columbia University Press.

Mearsheimer, John (1980) *Conventional Deterrence*, Ithaca, NY: Cornell University Press.

Medvedev, Zhores (1986) *Gorbachev*, Boston, MA: Little, Brown.

Morrison, John (1991) *Yeltsin: Bolshevik or Democrat?*, New York: Dutton.

Moynahan, Brian (1976) *Claws of the Bear: The History of the Red Army From the Revolution to the Present*, Boston, MA: Houghton Mifflin.

Myagkov, Aleksei (1976) *Inside the KGB*, New Rochelle, NY: Arlington House.

Nogee, Joseph and Robert Donaldson (1981) *Soviet Foreign Policy Since World War II*, New York: Pergamon.

Olson, Mancur (1977) *The Logic of Collective Action: Public Goods and the Theory of Groups*, Cambridge, MA: Harvard University Press.

—— (1982) *The Rise and Decline of Nations: Economic Growth, Stagflation, and Social Rigidities*, New Haven, CT: Yale University Press.

Peters, Ralph (1989) *Red Army*, New York: Pocket Books.

Remnick, David (1993) *Lenin's Tomb: The Last Days of the Soviet Empire*, New York: Random House.

Roxburgh, Angus (1993) *The Second Russian Revolution: The Struggle for Power in the Kremlin*, Cambridge, UK: Cambridge University Press.

Rubinstein, Alvin (1992) *Soviet Foreign Policy Since World War II*, 4th edn, New York: HarperCollins.

Seaton, Albert and Joan Seaton (1986) *The Soviet Army: 1918 to the Present*, New York: New American Library.

Scott, Harriet and William Scott (1984) *The Armed Forces of the USSR*, 3rd edn, revised and updated. Boulder, CO: Westview.

Shevardnadze, Eduard (1991) *The Future Belongs to Freedom*, New York: Free Press.

Sodaro, Michael (1990) *Moscow, Germany, and the West from Khrushchev to Gorbachev*, Ithaca, NY: Cornell University Press.

Steele, Jonathan (1984) *Soviet Power: The Kremlin's Foreign Policy from Brezhnev to Chernenko*, rev. edn, New York: Simon & Schuster.

Suvorov, Viktor (1984) *Inside the Soviet Army*, New York, Berkley.

Szabo, Stephen (1992) *The Diplomacy of German Unification*, New York: St. Martin's Press.

Talbott, Strobe (1985) *Deadly Gambits: The Reagan Administration and the Stalemate in Nuclear Arms Control*, New York: Vintage.

—— and Michael Beschloss (1993) *At the Highest Levels: The Inside Story of the End of the Cold War*, Boston, MA: Little, Brown.

Terry, Sarah (1983) *Soviet Policy in Eastern Europe*, New Haven, CT: Yale University Press.

Thompson, William (1989) *On Global War: Historical–Structural Approaches to World Politics*, Columbia, SC: University of South Carolina Press.

Vigor, P. H. (1983) *Soviet Blitzkrieg Theory*, New York: St. Martin's.

Waltz, Kenneth (1979) *Theory of International Politics*, Reading, MA: Addison-Welsley.

Werth, Alexander (1964) *Russia at War, 1941–1945*, New York: Dutton.

Wettig, Gerhard (1991) *Changes in Soviet Policy Towards the West*, Boulder, CO: Westview.

White, Stephen (1993) *After Gorbachev*, 4th edn, Cambridge, UK: Cambridge University Press.

Woodby, Sylvia and Alfred Evans, Jr (eds) (1990) *Restructuring Soviet Ideology: Gorbachev's New Thinking*, Boulder, CO: Westview.

Zaloga, Steven (1989) *Red Thrust: Attack on the Central Front*, Novato, CA: Presidio.

Ziegler, David (1987) *War, Peace and International Politics*, Boston, MA: Little, Brown.

Foreign Publications

Brandenburg, Ulrich (1992) *The "Friends" Are Leaving: Soviet and Post-Soviet Troops in Germany*, Cologne: Bundesinstitut fur Ostwissenschaftlich und International Studien.

"Encounter at Stavrapallo," *The Economist*, July 21, 1990 pp. 47–8.

Gorbachev, Mikhail (1987) *For a "Common European Home," For a New Way of Thinking*, Moscow: Novosti Press Agency.

"Gorbatschow kritisiert Honecker: Stasi nauppelt Verzwerfelte nieder," *Die Welt*, October 9, 1989, p. 1.

Ivanov, S. P. (1974) *Nachalnyi Period Voiny*, Moscow: Voyenizdat.

Krenz, Egon (1990) *Wenn Mauren Fallen*, Vienna: Paul Neff Verlag.

Sieren, Frank and Ludwig Koehe (eds) (1990) *Das Politburo,* Hamburg: Rohwohlt Taschenbuch Verlag.

Tomforde, Anna, "German Pullout 'Will Continue,'" *The Guardian* (August 20, 1991) p. 4.

Vor Der Spaltung, 1945–1991: Eine Deutsche Chronik in Texten und Bildern, Bonn: Presse und Informationsamt der Bundesreierung (1992).

"Wohin mit den Russen? 363 000 Sowjetsoldaten in der DDR," *Der Spiegel* (July 16, 1990) pp. 26–36.

Government Documents

Central Intelligence Agency (1990) *Atlas of Eastern Europe, August 1990*, Washington, DC: USGPO.

Department of Defense (1988) *Soviet Military Power, 1988: An Assessment of the Threat*, Washington, DC: USGPO.

—— (1989) *Soviet Military Power, 1989: Prospects for Change*, Washington, DC: USGPO.

Foreign Broadcast Information Services. *Daily Reports: Eastern Europe*, 1984–94.

—— *Daily Reports: Soviet Union*, 1986–94.

—— *Daily Reports: Western Europe*, 1989–94.

Newspapers

Financial Times, 1992–94.
New York Times, 1980–94.
Neues Deutschland, 1988–90.
Pravda, 1988–89.
Washington Post, 1991–94.

Index